ONCE
MY NAME WAS
SARA

A MEMOIR

I. Betty Grebenschikoff

ONCE MY NAME WAS SARA

First edition published in 1993

Published by Original Seven Publishing Company
P.O.Box 2249, Ventnor, New Jersey, 08406-2249

Printed by Cape Printing, Cape May, New Jersey

Library of Congress Catalog Card Number 93-86921

ISBN: 0-9639344-0-6

Manufactured in the United States of America

For my children

Jennifer, Sandy, Irene, Peter
and Nina, too

FU
(Blessing)

Cover photograph shows my German children's
identification document issued in 1939.

The name "Sara" appears on back cover.

Table of Contents

PREFACE

A few years ago I started to write a few stories about my childhood. I had no idea I would wind up with a book. But once I had begun to unlock the gates to memories carefully stored away, untouched for years, I found that I could not close them again. Telling the story had become an irresistible force. It took over my life. It would not let me go. And so I let it lead me, to places and people long ago, far away, along some paths that were pleasant, and some paths that were not.

Thinking yourself back to events that happened many years ago, is a very individual and selective process. There are many others who have gone through experiences similar to mine. It is quite possible that some of their recollections of shared events may be somewhat different. Everyone has their own built in system of dealing with the past. This book was written entirely from my personal viewpoint of life as I saw it, as I remember it. Not necessarily the one and only version of a period in time, it is, however, my version - and mine alone.

I owe thanks to my sister Edith, whose unfailingly steadfast support has meant so much in my life. Gently prodding her into remembering events from our childhood, always resulted in some shared laughter or tears. Her memories proved invaluable to me, her viewpoint of our shared life always realistic and candid.

My children have my love, as always, for their total support and constant encouragement for this venture. "Let's get on with it Ma, you can do it!" their battle cry, when at times I thought I would never make it through.

My husband Oleg, deserves several medals for patience and fortitude during the writing of this book. Enlisting his assistance at all hours of the day and night, for technical help with our computer, having "the book" take over much of my time and energy; nothing ever bothered him.   He remained enthusiastic, helpful and encouraging   throughout. Thank you, my dear.

I would like to thank my faithful mentor and trusted friend, Constance Quarterman Bridges, for volunteering to edit the manuscript.   Her thoughtful comments and objective criticism have been of immeasurable value.   With her considerable expertise and keen insight, she has helped to shape a book from a manuscript.

My thanks also to Karen M. Peluso, photographer and friend.   With dedication and skill, she has brought back to life the old photographs reproduced in this book.   I am grateful for her enthusiasm and unfailing support.

I. Betty Grebenschikoff

My identity card issued by International Committee for Refugees. Shanghai.

1. A GIFT FOR JENNIFER

D on't even think of buying me a birthday present this year," Jennifer, my oldest daughter, announces emphatically. Without unpacking her things, we have walked straight down to the beach. She is on her annual visit home. Her two boys are already building sand castles with their grandfather.

"Share the old family photographs with me. Let me read Opa's diary, or show me some of the letters you kept to yourself all this time." The June sun is warm on our faces, but our feet are pleasantly cool as we walk along the water's edge, scattering seagulls congregating in the sand in front of us.

I smile, there is so much to say, to think, to write. My life has been completely different from anything my children could ever have imagined. For a long time, I have carefully locked my memories somewhere in the back of my mind. Now I will have to find the key to let them all come out again. It will take courage. Maybe more courage than I have.

It is said that the greatest gift you can give to others, especially to your family, is the gift of self. A sense of awareness of who you are, where you came from, and the many events and people that shaped your life and made you

1

the person you are. Then maybe, just maybe, you may also recognize the direction you have chosen for yourself.

When our children were growing up, we lived for several years in Brigantine, New Jersey, in a house half a block away from the beach. It was always windy out there. Coming onto the island, over the bridge from Atlantic City, you could feel the difference in temperature and smell the fresh sea air right away. In summer the ocean breezes brought welcome relief from the heat; in sharp contrast to the freezing winds of winter. In our beds at night, we could hear the sound of the waves and smell the salty air coming into our open windows, as the wind whistled around corners of the house.

It was a perfect place to bring up our family. In those days, Brigantine was a quiet little island, with one traffic light, one public and one parochial school, a small shopping section and a trim looking Town Hall and library. It was the home of several thousand year round residents, who generally went off the island to work in near-by Atlantic City or the mainland communities. In summer, the population tripled with the influx of vacationers.

We came to this place after years of renting various rapidly shrinking apartments for our fast growing family. There we lived happily in our two-story house, complete with mortgage, big backyard with barbecue pit, sandbox and swings, plus various cats of uncertain pedigree in residence.

Every day in summer, we all climbed over the dunes making our way through the waving grass, ran into the ocean to swim, and played games on the beach. In winter, everyone bundled up and walked along the windswept shore. We all have the proverbial sand in our shoes. Now, a generation later, we take our grandchildren to another beach, a short distance up the coast, in Ventnor, and play the same games with them.

On a Sunday afternoon, we go to the Smithville Inn Craft Fair. We wander around looking at the displays of homemade articles. Mingled smells of hot dogs, sauerkraut and beer hang heavy in the air. It is one of the first hot days of summer. We drink sodas and take our sweaters off. We buy a balloon for the youngest grandchild, Celina, who is holding on to my hand. She sees the dolls for sale and wants to take them all home, to add to her collection.

I listen to the brass band under the big tent. Dressed in *lederhosen* and *dirndl* dresses they play and sing old German songs. The audience hums along with them. Something stirs in my memory. It is gone before I can catch it, like some half remembered dream. Some mornings, I lie very still and try to fall asleep again, to make a dream return. But only if it was a good dream. The bad ones come back anyway, uninvited, unwanted companions of the night.

A painting catches my eye.

"We don't need another picture of the beach," my husband informs me. "We have no wall space left, with all the photographs hanging everywhere."

I ask him which one he would do without, and he does not know.

The painting shows a beach, dune grass waving in the breeze. Puffy clouds over a calm sea, breakers rolling gently onto shore. The colors are sunset shades of blue and pink. Seagulls, lazily circling around, are ready to fly home for the night. How many? I count five seagulls.

I buy the picture and send it off to Jennifer. She will have her birthday present after all.

3

2. COFFEE AND CIGARS

My grandfather, Philip, often stopped in on Sunday mornings, when I was growing up in Berlin, to take me for a walk with him. The destination was usually his favorite coffee-house at the far end of Tiergarten Park. He sat in the kitchen chatting with my mother, waiting for me to be buttoned into my navy blue coat with matching hat. Then he took me by the hand, as we waved goodbye to Mutti, and off we went.

For some reason, the walks I remember best, were the ones we took on sunny autumn days, when there was a slight chill in the air. In my mind, I clearly see the leaves lazily drifting down from tall old trees in the park. I laughed and ran through brilliant piles of red and brown, scattering leaves in all directions, not caring that my good Sunday shoes and long white stockings became all spotted and wet. There was a damp cool smell of earth, grass and leaves all around. In the distance church bells pealed, while sparrows chattered in the trees nearby.

My grandfather, watching me, chuckled, as I chased the squirrels, who were busily collecting nuts to last them through the winter. High above, I heard the rush of wings and the lonesome sound of honking geese and ducks flying southward. After we walked all the way to the other side of the park, Opa headed for the coffee-house. A smell of coffee and cigars enveloped us as we walked through the door. Opa always ordered children's coffee for me. It consisted of a glass of malt coffee liberally diluted with sweetened hot milk, topped with

4

whipped cream sprinkled with cinnamon. He sat next to me at the little round table, sipping his coffee laced with brandy.

"Something to take off the chill," he explained, his blue eyes which were so much like my mother's, twinkling behind his pince-nez. He smoked his cigar, while he asked me how I was doing in school and whether I gave my teachers any trouble.

To this day, the sweet special smell of a certain blend of tobacco can take me right back to that coffee-house. I can almost hear the laughter, the clatter of coffee cups, the snapping sound of someone shaking out the Sunday newspapers that hung on wooden racks along the wall.

Everyone knew my grandfather. His friends came over to our table to pass the time of day and discuss the latest news. They patted me on the head or pinched my cheek and remarked how much I had grown since the last time they saw me. Sometimes they gave me coins to put in my piggy bank at home.

After a while, Opa pulled out his gold pocket watch from his vest pocket, and said it was time to go home. He put his derby on his head and shrugged into his heavy overcoat. I quickly finished my coffee, scraping out the last bit of sugar on the bottom of the glass with my spoon. Hand in hand we walked out into the cool autumn air.

3. LOOKING BACK

Dare I go back? Will it be too painful, or will it be a relief to let it all come back again? So much easier just to go on day by day, to live in the present. Try to forget those bygone years, let the memories lie untouched. But the challenge becomes too strong.

Getting started seems to me to be the biggest hurdle. For a long time now, I have been organizing my thoughts and memories, making an effort to put things in order. Trying to think myself back to the days of my childhood. It is all there in my head somewhere. All I have to do is to pull it out.

In the corner of my bedroom sits the box with old photo albums. My father's last diary is there, his army medals from the first World War, old passports and papers, odds and ends collected over many years. They gather dust.

"Come, look at us," they silently beckon, "we've been here waiting for you. We can take you back."

That sounds like a dangerous call. Siren songs across the water. I feel like an unwary fisherman, submerging my thoughts into the past, recalling people and places long gone.

At random I open one of the frayed albums. A picture of my grandparents looks at me. They sit side by side on a park bench, looking intently into someone's camera. I see a familiar expression on my grandmother's face. Glancing into the mirror, I realize that I recognize myself. There is some truth to the old biblical saying that the generations are linked one to another. It seems to me that the ones who have gone on before us, deserve some recognition, other than a fleeting moment in someone's memory, or a candle lit once a year.

Too many of my family have left no outward trace, no tombstones in old graveyards, not even records in some dusty Town Hall. They perished in the holocaust. Some alone, some with their families. They died in labor camps, or mass graves, reduced to ashes in places with hard to pronounce names, which are now familiar to the world. But all that came later, much later.

4. DITHA AND ILLE

I was born in Berlin in 1929, two years after my sister Edith. Within the family circle, Edith was always called by her pet name, Ditha, just as I was called Ille rather than Ilse. This was elevated to Dithimaus and Illemaus on those occasions when everyone was in a good mood, or we must have been extra well behaved, even if only for a short time.

After her marriage to my father, my mother left her secretarial job. She thoroughly enjoyed making a home, first for my father and then for all of us, as our family grew.

My father did a lot of traveling, all over Europe, for his company. He was employed by a stationery firm by the name of Schroeder Nachfolger. After being with the company for over twenty-five years, he had worked his way up to be one of their top salesmen.

Every year, Edith and I received our Chanukah presents from Herr Wollstein, my father's boss. They were always the same. Two long white boxes containing identical winter dresses, usually in dark blue wool with little lace collars and cuffs. They would lie hidden under my parents' bed until the first night of Chanukah, when they were pulled out to join our other presents. The dresses were always saved to wear as our best outfits for that year.

From my parents we always received a fancy box filled with a selection of nuts, candies and oranges. In addition, there was sometimes a doll or a book, or something special that we wanted. My mother used to cover all the presents that were on the table, with a large cloth. After the candles were lit on the Menorah, she pulled the cloth away and there,

8

to our delight, were our presents.

Our last apartment in Berlin, the one I remember best, was a rambling, comfortable place at Siegmundshof 13 in Tiergarten. Edith and I shared a large sunny room. I remember the wallpaper on the walls. Blue cornflowers repeating themselves endlessly around the room. My books and dolls were lined up on the dresser. Edith was always interested in gardening. Her little flowerpots filled with hyacinths stood on the white tiled windowsill.

The apartment had a long corridor, that seemed to contain a lot of mysterious shadows at night, especially before you finally got to the light switch, located at the far end. I was afraid of the dark, so I used to run through as fast as I could, hoping that nothing horrible would catch me.

This feeling became even more intense, when I read the German version of *The Hound of the Baskervilles*. After that, before I ventured out of my room, I always called out: "Somebody please switch on the light for me." My economical parents were in the habit of turning lights off behind them. This was one habit I would not get into when I grew up, I promised myself.

The corridor led to my parents' bedroom, and then on to my father's library, with the heavy brown leather armchairs around his writing table. There was a radio in that room, up on the shelf surrounded by his books. A little sculpture of a cat stood near the window. At night when the lights were out, that statue glowed with a greenish light. It must have been treated with something to retain light. Sometimes I asked permission to borrow it. Then I would crawl under the feather quilt covering my bed and watch it glow.

Our kitchen had a little pantry, stocked with jars of fruit

and vegetable preserves my mother put up, and an old fashioned icebox with a block of ice in it. Kasimir, our parakeet, sat in his cage on the sunny windowsill singing to the birds outside in the garden. My father taught him to whistle a six note family whistle. Pappi liked to announce his arrival home with fanfare. He also used it to get our attention, when we were outdoors. It instantly brought Edith and me running to him.

I spent many hours sitting at the scrubbed kitchen table, supervised by my mother; drawing or doing my homework, contentedly munching on a snack she had prepared for me. I was considered a fussy eater at mealtimes, but I always loved to eat slices of rye bread spread with butter, after I came home from school.

At the end of the corridor there was a large formal dining room with dark carved furniture. A Persian carpet partially covered the parquet floor. Crystal bowls filled with fruit, stood on the sideboard, next to thin-stemmed wine glasses in brilliant colors of blue, red, green and amber. They sparkled like jewels, when they caught the sunlight coming in through the french doors, leading to a large balcony. The landscaped garden of the apartment complex, where we always played, was just beyond.

In the summertime, we used to eat our meals out on the balcony, sitting around a table covered with a red and white polka dot waxed tablecloth. My mother and my sister always kept the window boxes all along the railing, filled with a profusion of flowers. It felt as though we had our own little garden, a special private place just for us.

5. THE MUELLERS

My mother's parents, Philip and Jeanette Mueller, lived within walking distance from us, in Charlottenburg, on the third floor of an old Weitzstrasse apartment building. We visited them often. Edith and I used to play hide and seek there, while my mother sat and talked with my grandmother. My favorite hiding place was under my grandparents' high old-fashioned bed. I knew that if I crawled right underneath the middle of the bed, Edith could see me but never reach me.

Compared to all the soups I ever tasted, my grandmother's potato soup was undoubtedly the best. An aromatic broth, with chunks of potatoes and carrots, and as always, freshly chopped parsley sprinkled on top. Crusty home baked bread, liberally spread with butter, was always eaten along with the soup. It was a special treat for us to sit in her kitchen, or in good weather, on her little balcony overlooking the courtyard, and eat from her large white soup plates, using the heavy old silver spoons handed down from my great-grandmother.

It was not until I was much older, that I realized why my grandmother cooked potato soup so often. It was cheap and nourishing, and probably it was all she could afford. My grandfather was a charming man with a wonderful personality and good looks, always full of jokes and fun. However, I suspect, being the greatest provider was probably not among his attributes. He was an upholsterer and decorator by trade, but jobs were not always plentiful. He liked to spend his spare time in the coffee-house with his cronies, playing cards {Skat}, drinking Slivovitz and smoking his ever present cigar. With Hungarian blood in his veins, he sometimes had a hot temper. Whenever I disagreed with anybody, I was always reminded, that I inherited this character trait directly from him.

He adored my grandmother, called her his Jenny, and always treated her with the greatest respect. For many years her mother, whose name was Bettina Rabinowicz, also lived with them. She died when I was very young. I have faint memories of her as a tall dignified lady, wearing her hair pulled up in a bun. She always wore long black dresses and prayed a lot.

My grandmother Jeanette, whom we called Omi, had a beautiful clear complexion and wavy light brown hair. She wore light print dresses in summer and dark woolen ones, with hand crocheted lace collars, in the winter.

I liked to climb on her ample lap and snuggle up to her, breathing in the faint scent of her 4711 Eau de Cologne, feeling very safe and warm in her arms. To this day it is the only perfume I ever use. She never minded, when I used to braid the long fringes, that hung down from the paisley satin tablecloth on her living room table. Something my mother usually scolded me for, when she noticed it.

Once, Omi took me along to a Bar-Mitzvah of a second cousin named Heinz. Afterwards, there was coffee and cake with the family. I fervently hoped that no one would take my favorite pastry, which I spied immediately upon entering the dining room. It was a marzipan basket filled with apricot jam. Since my Omi was the oldest person there, she naturally had first choice, and sure enough she chose the marzipan basket.

"Don't make such a long face, Illemaus," she whispered softly to me, "here, I took it for you." Later when she fell and broke her hip, we visited her in the hospital and brought her flowers. After that, she rarely left her apartment, and used a cane to help her get around.

My mother had two sisters. The older one, Tante Grete, lived nearby, with her husband, Onkel Martin Baer. Being childless, they both worked. In their spare time, they enjoyed all kinds of sports. Long walks and gymnastics, followed by a cold shower, was a way of life with them.

They owned a little sailboat. On weekends they used to go sailing on Wannsee. Sometimes Edith and I were invited to go with them. They always packed their lunch of sandwiches, potato salad with frankfurters and a thermos with something hot in it. No matter what it was, it always tasted wonderful, eating picnic style on the water.

The younger sister Alice, referred to as Tante Liccie, also lived in Berlin, with her husband Onkel Erwin Koeppler. My uncle had a little cigar and newspaper store, my aunt was a secretary in an office. They had a gramophone in their living room, on which my uncle liked to play German operettas for us. He always had a joke or a magic trick, ready to make us laugh. We called him our Magic Uncle.

In later years when Edith and I were both married and had children, he continued to play the same jokes and tricks on them. They loved it as much as we did. How did he find the coin behind our ears, when he just had it in his pocket?

Like us, my uncle and aunt also owned a parakeet. His name was Pippifax. This bird had learned to say his name and address. One day he escaped through the open window and landed on someone else's window sill. He identified himself, was promptly returned to my delighted uncle and aunt, and put back in his cage. The Berlin newspapers printed the story. My uncle carried the clipping of it in his wallet for

13

years.

The youngest of the family was my mother's brother, Ernst Mueller, known as Bobby within the family. Nobody could remember why his name was Bobby. He was tall, with dark wavy hair, blue eyes like my mother, and had a brilliant smile. He was a salesman for a men's store and always had many girlfriends. He used to bring them to our house quite often, usually around dinner time. Edith and I would bet whether he would marry this one or that one.

In the years before 1938, when Jews were still allowed to travel freely, our family sometimes went to Swinemuende, on the Baltic Sea, during the summer vacation. My father rented a wind shelter for us on the beach. After romping about in the cold water, we quickly wrapped ourselves in our multi-colored striped bath robes. They always felt so cozy and warm.

We used to rent rooms at a boarding house, near the beach at Swinemuende. The landlady, Frau Tomas, was a tall, thin lady, without a single tooth in her mouth. Edith and I were awe-struck. We had never seen anything like this before. I had a habit, in those days, of not smiling at anyone and wearing a ferocious expression. This, together with my bright red hair, caused Frau Tomas to refer to me, as the little devil with the evil eye.

For two summers, before we left Germany, my parents rented a little vacation cottage outside Berlin, in a place called Schoenblick. It was peaceful out there in the country. In Berlin, Edith and I always wore dresses, but in Schoenblick all we wore were our shorts, sleeveless shirts, and our brown sandals. Edith always got a nice suntan, while I collected ever more freckles.

The cottage was near a forest. The wind blowing through

the trees would sing us to sleep at night. We had a large garden to play in, also a big sand box at the far end, where we spent many happy hours digging in the cool, soft sand.

My mother's family often came to visit by train, from Berlin, on weekends. They liked to take long walks in the woods or pick wild berries. My mother was kept busy feeding all of them. She usually lay down with a migraine after everyone left. Boiled potatoes, fresh asparagus and scrambled eggs were a staple summer meal cooked in the little kitchen, where the bees and flies were buzzing around, getting themselves imprisoned on curling, sticky strips of paper hanging from the ceiling. The men played cards outside, at a table set up in the garden, and the women sat together, knitting, drinking coffee and eating pastries, laughing and gossiping.

I remember one hot summer afternoon, when Edith and I decided that we did not like Onkel Ernst's latest flame, because she kept teasing us. This one was a plump young woman, dressed in a blue silk dress, whom we had to address as Tante Fanny. We crept up behind her and Edith drenched the poor girl with the garden hose. Punishment was swiftly administered and Edith was sent to her room, even though she swore it was all an accident.

Onkel Ernst did not marry that one, or maybe she lost interest, once she got herself dried out, and he had stopped laughing.

6. CZECHOSLOVAKIA.

In the middle 1930's, when I was about six or seven years old, we spent a summer visiting my father's family, the Kohns. That was the first and last time I ever saw my Czechoslovakian grandparents, and most of the other family members who lived there.

My father had taken my mother to Teschen, after they were first married, to get acquainted with his parents, sisters and brothers, but with the exception of my father's older sister Tante Irma, we children were not familiar with that side of the family. Tante Irma, who was divorced from her husband, visited us occasionally in Berlin. Sometimes she stayed with us for several weeks. Edith and I always enjoyed her visits, we liked to listen to the stories she made up for us. She had two sons, who also came sometimes, but we were not very close as they were much older than we were.

Adolf and Rosalie Kohn had nine children. My father was the second child in their family of five boys and four girls. By the time we visited them, that summer, they had already lost three of their children. Fritz had disappeared in Russia, during the first World War. Another brother, named Otto, had died in infancy. A sister, Julie, committed suicide, when she was quite young. It seems there was an unhappy love affair with a Polish officer, but the details were sketchy and no one talked about it. I know though that my father kept her in his memory. Near the end of his life, when his thoughts sometimes wandered, he often called me Julie. I used to make him laugh, when I told him that if he called me Julie, I would

16

call him Charlie.

The remaining five brothers and sisters gave our family a huge welcome. They were all married and had children, so we were surrounded by our newfound cousins. One of them was a little boy about my age called Peter, with whom I fell in love right away. Both of us had some of the characteristics of the Kohn family. Brown eyes with that downward slant, red hair and freckles. I wished he were my brother, and told my parents I wanted him to come home with me. We were quite inseparable. I was very upset when we had to leave him at the end of our visit.

When I first saw my grandparents, I felt that I already knew them. They looked so much like the photographs we had of them at home. It was also interesting to see how much my father looked like his parents. He had the same brown eyes and facial structure as his father. From his mother, he inherited his full lips and the way she puckered her mouth. My mother always jokingly referred to this likeness as his *Kohnische Ponem*.

The whole family contributed their efforts for our first family meal in my grandparents' apartment. A long table was set, reaching from one room into the next, covered with a white tablecloth, set with their finest silver, china and long-stemmed crystal wine glasses. The dishes kept coming out of the kitchen filled with chicken noodle soup, heaped platters of *goulash* and *nockerl*, roast goose, red cabbage with apples, poppy seed noodles, *tzimmes*, homebaked *challah*, apple and *mohn strudels*, almond cakes and on and on. I remember my grandmother got so excited, that when she finally sat down at the table, she missed her chair and landed on the floor. That caused a lot of commotion, of course, and some quickly

17

suppressed giggles from the children, but fortunately she was not hurt.

After the initial welcome, we spent several weeks visiting with different members of the family. Tante Hermine and Onkel Emil had a son named Otto, and a younger child about Edith's age, a beautiful girl with dark curly hair. Her name was Lydia. She and my sister became fast friends. I spent a lot of time playing with cousin Peter and another young cousin, Herbert.

We all took outings into the beautiful Tatra mountains with our relatives. My father wanted to show us all the places where he had grown up. There was constant joking and laughing going on. My mother had a good sense of humor, fitting right in with that whole high spirited family. My uncles, who thought my mother quite fascinating, could not do enough for her and flattered her continuously. Naturally, she enjoyed this. My father, far from feeling any jealousy, just beamed with pride.

My aunts, all quite modishly dressed, decided that my hairstyle was out of fashion and should be changed from the bangs I had always worn, to parting my hair over to the side. They put a big white silk bow in my hair and I remember feeling very good about myself. I loved the fuss they made over me.

Eventually we went back to Berlin by train. The whole family came to see us off. There were the grandparents, our cousins, the uncles, the aunts, many of them wiping tears from their eyes. Leaning out of the carriage windows, we waved to them, shouting our last good-byes.

Almost all of them were rounded up by the Germans a few years later, deported and killed in the ghettos and extermination camps of Poland.

There were only three survivors that we know of. One of them was Tante Irma, the oldest sister. No longer young or in very good health, she somehow managed to survive several years of internment in various concentration camps. She was a victim of medical experiments by Nazi doctors. Upon liberation from the camps, she lived for some time in Prague, with her brother Artur, who also miraculously survived. His wife and children were killed.

After the war, when we found out that she was still alive, my father often wrote to her and helped finance her trip to Israel. There, Tante Irma made her home with one of her sons for a few years, before she finally died in an Israeli hospital.

Our older cousin Otto Borger, whom we had visited that summer in Teschen, was another survivor of the camps. He lost his entire family and his fiancee in the concentration camps. Later, he also settled in Israel and re-established contact with our family. Otto was particularly close to my father, with whom he exchanged letters for many years.

7. THE FARINA STORY.

The fine art of eating was always considered a serious business, when I was growing up. Not only was it a time when the whole family gathered together, but it was also expected, that you showed your appreciation for the food, how it was cooked, and more importantly, by whom it was cooked and served.

From early childhood, Edith and I were taught to help my mother in the kitchen. I generally wound up peeling potatoes, a task at which I could do the least damage, while Edith was promoted to more interesting work, as she showed more aptitude in the kitchen than I ever did. We were expected to make pleasant conversation at mealtimes, and finish what was on our plates, with constant reminders to think about unfortunate children, who had less than we did. Even with that thought in mind, I was often the last one remaining at the table, dawdling or looking for a place to hide my vegetables. I could never understand how I did those poor children any good, by forcing myself to eat something awful, like liver or spinach, when I hated it so much.

Special foods though, were often subtly entwined with family legends. Take the case of farina, or *Griesbrei* as we used to call it. Without question this was our favorite food. It was definitely not just an ordinary dish of hot cereal. There were absolute rules and regulations, concerning the preparation and style of eating, this always delectable dish.

The ceremony of the farina had been handed down in the family to become a fine art. Various family members have been known to get into heated discussions on this subject, each claiming to be the absolute expert.

"First of all you have to cook it slowly in boiling milk, keep stirring all the time," my mother intones with authority, "never use a bowl, but pour the farina onto a flat plate. Pour melted butter over it, sprinkle with sugar and don't forget the cinnamon."

We smile in anticipation, our mouths already watering. From the time we were little, Edith and I know, that you start eating it from the outer edges, slowly turning the plate in a circle. Any uninitiated soul hardy enough to put their spoon into the middle of the plate, finds out very quickly, that you burn your mouth that way.

My father liked to tell us stories of his childhood in Baumgarten. The farina story was always one of our favorites. We always begged him to tell it to us just one more time. Complaining just enough, but secretly pleased, he would comply.

"Look, I cooked it especially for you. Eat it up. A little more cinnamon, maybe?" Her kindly voice pleaded with him.

"Please mother, I can't, not another spoonful. I must go." My father protested, while his mother fussed about him trying to keep him there just a little longer.

"I was a reluctant soldier," he continued. "I was involved in a war I neither understood nor wanted to take part in. I liked the quiet peaceful things of life, my nature was never one of a fighter. But I had no choice, I was drafted. Just before I left my parents' house to join my regiment, my mother cooked my favorite dish of farina for me."

"Now, you know that I went off to war without finishing everything on my plate, I was just too full," my father continued with the familiar story, as we moved closer, so as not to miss a word.

"Within the first week my regiment got lost in the field. We were cold, hungry and wet, rations were short. We were miserable. All I could think of was that unfinished dish of farina. It absolutely haunted me. I could almost hear my mother's pleading voice. I would have given anything at that point to be back in her warm kitchen and taste again that hot, buttery, fragrant ambrosia. It seemed infinitely more precious than the fanciest meal I could imagine."

Well, my father survived that war, and the next one too. He lived to a ripe old age, still enjoying his daily helping of *Griesbrei*. His children and grandchildren grew up and often cooked the same thing for themselves, not deviating from the time honored tradition of course.

Sometimes when I smell the fragrance of cinnamon mixed with hot butter, it almost seems as if Pappi, or Opa as the grandchildren called him, is right there in the kitchen with me.

8. MAX AND OLGA KOHN.

M y parents met in Berlin in 1926, at a dance of *Die Getreuen*, (The Faithful), a Jewish social club. My father fell in love with my mother, with her vitality and gaiety, her blue eyes and stylishly bobbed black hair. She was eleven years younger than he.

Their wedding picture shows them standing on the steps of the *Berliner Standesamt*, (Registry Office). My mother is fashionably attired in a wool coat with fur trim, clutching a bouquet of roses. She is wearing a cloche type hat pulled low over her eyes, but there is no mistaking the big smile on her face. My father stands proudly next to her, attired in hat, gloves and coat. Actually it was a *paletot*. All his life, he referred to his coats by the French word *paletot*. Standing on either side, are my two grandfathers, Philip Mueller and Adolf Kohn.

When my father grew up, his family lived in the village of Baumgarten near the Austrian-Czechoslovakian border. His parents earned their living by running a small inn with an attached grocery store.

After serving in the German Army during the first World War, my father moved to Germany and eventually went to work in the stationery business in Berlin. He was a quiet, studious young man, not in the best of health due to a war injury. Never having gone to university he, nevertheless, amassed a wealth of knowledge by voraciously reading anything he could get his hands on, and using his inquiring mind wherever possible.

I inherited his brown eyes and reddish hair, but unfortunately not his calm, even temperament. No matter how much or how little money he earned, he never forgot his less fortunate relatives. He supported his parents in Czechoslovakia with monthly checks, in addition to helping his sisters and brothers out of many difficulties.

It was also routine for instance, that every Friday afternoon, my sister and I accompanied my mother on a trip to the grocery store. All of us carrying bulging, hand-knitted shopping bags, we walked to my mother's parents' apartment in Charlottenburg to visit, and just incidentally, re-stock the pantry.

My mother's family came from Austria, although my grandfather Philip, was a born Hungarian. When my mother was a little girl, Philip and Jeanette moved their family from Vienna to Berlin, in search of a better standard of living.

Growing up during the first World War, my mother, her sisters and brother were often hungry, when the neighborhood grocer refused to extend any more credit. With my grandfather off to the war and my grandmother working in a factory to make ends meet, times were hard for the family.

"I used to eat my girlfriend's ham sandwiches at school," my mother confided to us. "I knew we were not allowed to eat ham, but I was always so hungry, so I hoped that God would forgive me and my mother would not find out." She also spared her mother the news that she was picked to be the Christmas angel at the school play, mainly because she had the longest hair in the class and did not look too obviously Jewish, according to her teacher.

Fortunately her youth gave her a happy-go-lucky attitude and she tended to see the bright side of things. As the years went by, she often had a struggle to retain that optimism. She was a good athlete, a champion swimmer for her sports club, a wonderful dancer and had many boyfriends. She often reminisced, with my sister and I as her spellbound audience.

After they were married, she tried to get my father involved in sports, something at which he was hopelessly inadequate. Exercises left him breathless and sore, and swimming just about killed him.

"Your mother nearly drowned me," he laughingly told us. "She used to make faces at me while I was trying at least to stay afloat, so I laughed until I sank."

Always a good cook, she set about to put some meat on his skinny frame. She spent many hours in the kitchen cooking his favorite things, from Hungarian *goulash* to *Mehlspeisen,* which included apricot dumplings drenched in butter. *Mohnstriezel,* chicken soups swimming in fat, noodle puddings, *Muerbeteig* cookies; all these wonderful things came marching out of the kitchen at him.

She finally slowed down, when he gained too much weight and his gallbladder revolted. Then she made him take long walks with her, to get him back in shape again. Never one to complain or find fault with anything she did, he loved every minute of it. All he wanted was to be with her and make her happy. He often called her his little *Olinko,* his Czechoslovakian nickname for her.

THE BUMBLE BEE BALLET

When I was young
I went to dancing school.
Like bumble bees
we buzzed about.

And one two three,
and one two three.
My mother laughed so hard
the teacher made her
leave the room.

I looked at beauty
all around me,
I sensed
a symphony of sky
and wind and sun.

With spirits high
I heard the music
and danced with joy.
My mind so free.

But yet my feet,
and one two three,
and one two three,
had hardly left the ground.

9. ANNEMARIE

At home we spoke only German. We never considered ourselves different from the people around us. Edith and I were familiar with the German songs my mother used to sing to us. *Roeslein, Roeslein auf der Heide,* was one of her favorites, along with Strauss' Vienna waltzes with which she identified, being a born Viennese herself. She also liked to recite poetry out loud. Goethe and Schiller were among her favorites. Sometimes in fun she changed the words around, or used them in a different context. We never knew what to expect.

Some evenings, when the doorbell rang, she quoted: *Wer reitet so spaet durch Nacht und Wind?* (Who rides so late through night and wind?) a line from one of her favorite poems, *Der Erlkoenig.* Edith and I would giggle, as she opened the door to see who was there.

By tradition, we regularly went to synagogue services and also attended Jewish schools. Most of our friends were Jewish, but we were also quite friendly with some German children who lived near us. Contentedly we went on day by day, not for a moment did we feel that we did not belong exactly where we were at the time. My parents often went to the opera and concert halls with their friends. They took full advantage of the many cultural events Berlin had to offer.

As they became aware of the changes in German society, the officially approved anti-Semitism which gradually became more and more obvious, the many different rules and restrictions the government started to use against Jews, my parents, along with many others, hoped it was just a passing phase.

Trying to shield us from anything unpleasant, they never discussed anything in front of my sister and me. All we saw then was, that my mother acted a lot more nervous than before, and that our parents seemed to have a lot to talk about with our relatives, while we were sent out on some errand out of earshot.

My best friend, during that time, was a girl in my class called Annemarie Wahrenberg. We both disliked our teacher Fraulein Emmanuel with some intensity. She was a tall, thin woman wearing plain dark dresses and given to making long speeches on the virtues of honesty and truth.

When I was about six or seven years old, I broke my left arm while jumping over my sister's back, from my perch on the tabletop. I was doing my imitation of an airplane.

After six weeks, the cast was cut off by our family doctor, with my mother's poultry scissors. I was even required to thank him for this uncomfortable maneuver. Reluctantly, I mumbled: *"Danke schoen, Herr Doktor Gottschalk."*

Not long after that there was some petty thievery going on in the school. Naturally, we all swore up and down that we did not take the candy mysteriously missing from Fraulein Emmanuel's drawer. Not one to trust our protestations of innocence, Miss Honesty and Truth went through our schoolbags. My bag was quite heavy that day, beside my books there was also some unexplained candy. Staunchly I insisted that it had gotten there by itself.

Later that day, I ran to one of the benches in the playground and stretched out my recently healed left arm to save the place for Annemarie. A boy, whom I had never liked, and liked even less afterwards, promptly sat down on my arm. I felt something crack. And so here it was, back to the heavy gypsum cast for another six weeks. For years I was quite convinced, that breaking my arm the second time, was divine retribution for the candy heist.

Annemarie and I were inseparable. Once a week we took dancing lessons together, designed to teach us a measure of grace and balance. I don't know how successful that was, but we always had a good time at the studio, much to the amusement of our watching mothers. We played at each other's homes, freely letting our imaginations roam. Dressing up in old sheets and blankets, we would pretend to be American movie stars. We must have seen some American movies around that time.

"If you eat candy while sitting down and putting your feet on the table like the Americans do, you'll never get sick," declared Annemarie with authority.

I believed every word she said, and we often put this theory to the test, until our mothers caught up with us. I remember that as a special treat we went to the movies, whenever a new German-dubbed Shirley Temple, or a Laurel and Hardy movie, was playing. We firmly believed that anything we saw in the movies was absolutely real, and especially so if it was made in America.

Beside spending time with our own special friends, Edith and I often gathered with children living in our apartment building. We visited each other and played in the garden together, roller skating or comparing our doll carriages and discussing what our *babies* had been doing. I used to show off my doll clothes, all carefully handmade by my mother for my large doll family.

My father, an amateur photographer, often set up his tripod and posed us for pictures out there in the sunny back garden. Frequently, we were patted on the head by the neighbors and complimented on being such nice mannerly girls. We were taught to be respectful to our elders, to open doors for adults, and curtsey in the time honored European manner, when older people spoke to us.

However, gradually the neighbors stopped speaking to us. They looked the other way, when we met in the halls or in the garden. Doors were slammed in our faces. The children were not allowed to play with us anymore.

"Mutti, what did we do to them? They act as if they don't know us."

"Hush, not so loud! We are Jews, that's why. They are afraid of being reported to the police for talking to us."

"Dirty rotten Jews," our former playmates yelled at us, proudly dressed in their brand new Hitler Youth uniforms, festooned with swastikas. Still confused, we nevertheless very quickly learned to stay out of their way.

My parents, by then realizing the seriousness of the situation, finally sat down with us, and tried to explain what was happening in our lives and how best to protect ourselves. From now on we were to keep a low profile, not to talk back to anyone, come straight home from school and stay out of any controversy, no matter what we saw on the streets. If we could suddenly become invisible that would be even better, I thought to myself.

Early in 1939, during my third year at the private Jewish Community School I attended, the Germans requisitioned our building. All the pupils and teachers were forced to move into another already overcrowded Jewish School. My sister was also transferred there, from the school she attended then. Fortunately for us, this new school was located much closer to the apartment where we lived. This made our walk to and from school a little easier. We tried not to draw attention to ourselves, but sometimes we were pushed off the sidewalk by hooligans, who thought it was fun to throw stones at Jewish children and spit on them.

Every morning at roll call, the students gathered in the playground which was surrounded by a big stone fence. Every morning there were a few less students. Families who got permission to emigrate to other countries were leaving daily.

That spring, Annemarie's father was taken away by the Gestapo for questioning. She still attended school, but had become very quiet and withdrawn. I was not told anything and could not imagine what had happened. Whispered conversations by my parents were quickly interrupted, when I came into the room.

The last time I ever saw Annemarie was just before our family left Berlin. Our parents had arranged for us to meet in the school playground to say good-bye. Annemarie was accompanied by her father, who had just been released by the Germans. I did not recognize him. His hair had turned white and he looked like an old man. I was very frightened.

Annemarie and I said our farewells and swore to remember each other for ever and ever. I don't know if she and her parents were able to leave Germany. I never saw or heard from her again.

10. ONCE MY NAME WAS SARA

Smouldering anti-Semitism in Central Europe finally burst into full bloom, with the encouragement and active participation of the Hitler regime. Restrictions and penalties levied at Jews, so-called Aryanization of Jewish businesses and enterprises in Germany became more and more widespread, culminating with what came to be known as Crystal Night, in November of 1938. Hundreds of Jewish stores, homes and synagogues, were destroyed by the Nazis while the police looked the other way. In many cases, the authorities helped in the destruction, as well as taking part in beatings and abuse of Jewish people, who had the misfortune of being out on the streets that night.

Every pane of glass in our synagogue on Levetzostrasse was shattered. We used to go to this temple, with my parents, on the High Holidays and for Friday evening Shabbat services.

After the *Kiddush* was sung by the Cantor and the congregation, the children were always invited by the Rabbi to gather on the *Bimah*, where little glasses of grape juice were poured for us. We all stood in a row, drinking our *wine*, then we went back to sit with our parents, as the service continued.

The building was gutted, the prayer books and torahs with their embroidered velvet covers set on fire. The police, aided by mobs of hooligans, forced Jewish men and women to clean up the debris in the streets on their hands and knees. Several weeks later on the way to my grandparents' house, we walked by some of the looted Jewish shops and synagogues. We could still hear glass crunching beneath our feet.

Old confident beliefs of security and safety in the civilized world of German life and culture, were shattered along with the glass that night. That security proved to be just an illusion, was difficult for German Jews to comprehend at first. But the time had come to face reality. Nothing would ever be the same again.

Beginning on a small scale in 1933, Hitler's regime of terror escalated over the next few years. The assimilation of the Jews into German sciences, their contributions to musical, educational and cultural pursuits ended in arrests, persecution and death.

By the late thirties, my parents were desperately looking for ways to escape from Germany. Besides trying to get the family to safety, my father also tried to avoid the expected summons by the Gestapo. They were rounding up Jewish males for what was euphemistically known as "questioning." Frequently these sessions were followed by imprisonment.

"Well children, aren't we lucky. We are all getting new middle names." My father was still trying to appear optimistic, while at the same time my mother was in tears.

In the summer of 1938, another edict had been handed down by the Germans. It was the addition of the name Sara for Jewish females, and Israel, for Jewish males, to be used as legal middle names. All our papers had to be changed to the new names at the police station, to better identify us officially as Jews.

At the age of eight, the significance of this latest intentional degradation escaped me at the time.

I was fast becoming confused by all my names anyhow. My middle name of Margot was dropped for the time being. From my great-grandmother Bettina, I had inherited a third name, Betty. That name disappeared altogether for several years, until I resurrected it later when I was about sixteen.

According to the Germans, from now on I was officially Ilse Sara Kohn. My last two school report cards were made out in this new name. My teachers signed them, including their new middle names. However, my father ignored the whole business and sent my report cards back to school, using his original Max Kohn signature.

Emigrating to the United States or other desirable countries was difficult for us, as we did not have necessary quota numbers or visas. Born in Czechoslovakia, my father carried a *Fremdenpass*, which was an identity certificate for stateless people without a proper passport. This *Fremdenpass* had to be renewed punctually by the German Police. For reasons known only to themselves, the Germans did not choose stateless Jews for the concentration camps, when they first started with their selections. Later, no more exceptions were made.

Living in Berlin since he was a young man, my father fought for the Germans in the First World War. He never held a German passport and did not qualify for German quota numbers for immigration to the U.S.A. Not having a proper passport, he was also denied entry into many other countries. Beside all these problems, the fact remained that we did not have any relatives outside of Germany who could sponsor us anyway.

Jewish leaders urged their people to leave the country as soon as possible, or at least to send their children out of Germany. My sister and I were put on the list of the *Aliyah* children who were being sent out to Palestine.

These children became part of the early kibbutzim settlers of what later became the State of Israel. My cousin Heinz

Kohn whose Bar-Mitzvah I attended two years earlier, went to Palestine on one of these transports. As it turned out later, he was the only member of his family to survive the war. He told me his story some five decades later, when we re-established contact with each other.

Heinz became a volunteer soldier in the British Army in Palestine, when he was eighteen years old. He was to spend nearly five years in the army, serving in Egypt and Libya and was present at the Allied invasion in Salerno, Italy. During that time, his mother, Rosa, who was my maternal grandfather's sister, her husband Karl and a sister Lizzy were sent to Theresienstadt by the Germans. They did not survive. Heinz, whose Hebrew name is Seew, now lives in Israel with his wife Deborah, surrounded by their children and grandchildren.

Edith and I were all excited about leaving for Palestine. We belonged to a Theodore Hertzl Club in Berlin, where we learned to sing Hebrew pioneer songs. We had heard all about kibbutz life in sunny Palestine, where everyone lived and worked together, marching off into the fields to pick oranges, wearing little sunhats and waving blue and white flags. At least that was the way it looked in the picture books. It sounded good to us, we could not wait to pack our bags. But my mother did not want to split the family up. At the last moment, after much agonizing, she refused to let us go, afraid that she would never see us again. Her instinct was of course quite right, but we were rather disappointed that we were not going to be pioneers after all.

For a while it looked as though my father might be successful in getting us all out to South America. Spanish lessons by a tutor were started at home. The one phrase we all remembered was: "*Vaya con Dios, senor, pero vaya.*" In later years, this became a family joke. One of us would whisper it to the other, when a guest overstayed his welcome: "Go with God, Sir, but go."

The South American venture fell through and the Spanish tutor was quickly replaced by an English speaking one, just in case we could go somewhere where English was needed.

I remember waking up one night, that spring, when my Onkel Ernst came to say good-bye to us. His white scarf contrasted against his navy blue coat, as he stood in the dark corridor embracing my mother. Carrying only a small suitcase, and a summons from the Gestapo tucked in his pocket, he fled to Prague, where he had arranged to meet his fiancee, Martel. After a quick marriage ceremony, they went across to England, where they made a living hiring themselves out as a butler and maid team.

When the war was over they settled down in Nottingham. My uncle, by then known as an anglicized Ernest Miller, went into the insurance business, Aunt Martel operated a boarding house for many years.

Our family made several trips to the Berlin train station to say good-bye to friends and relatives. There was a distant cousin whose name was Ilse, just like mine. She was from the Koeppler family and was being sent out to England along with a group of Jewish children. Her navy blue beret jammed over her straight brown hair, she waved to us out of the train window, until we could not see her anymore. She survived the war, living with an English family, who later adopted her. Her sister, Marianne, was a nurse and was not allowed to leave by the authorities. The Germans used her to work in their hospitals during the early part of the war. Later she was sent to her death in a concentration camp, along with her parents.

As more and more countries refused entry to us, it finally became clear to my parents, that the one place left for us to save our lives was China. Many thousands of miles away, accessible only by a long sea voyage, it was a totally different country whose climate, oriental environment and questionable political and economic outlook, not to mention the language problem, was largely unknown to us. Shanghai was, however, the one spot where European Jews were permitted to land without a visa, affidavit, or certificate of guaranty, considered so necessary by other countries.

The Japanese shipping company, *Nippon Yusen Kaisha*, whose ships sailed to the Orient, gave my father a negative reply, when he tried to buy tickets for a sailing to Shanghai. They were booked for months ahead. However, when my father returned again and pleaded with them to re-examine his papers, which incidentally also contained 500 German Marks for the shipping officer folded inside, the reply was more hopeful.

A few days later, my father received a telephone call with the good news. Two first class cabins were reserved for us on the *Kashima Maru*, sailing from Naples to Shanghai, on May 21, 1939.

11. THE LIFT

In preparation for our journey to China, the whole family was outfitted with new clothes suitable to the tropical climate in Shanghai. My parents acted as though we were going on safari to the end of the world.

"Better safe than sorry. You never know what you might need," was my father's opinion.

Attempts at selling some of our things were only partially successful, as the Aryan customers were afraid to be seen buying anything from Jews.

A Berlin shipping company delivered a huge wooden crate, known in family circles as The Lift. Excepting our hand luggage and whatever could be packed into two steamer trunks, which accompanied us on the *Kashima Maru*, everything else we wanted to take to China, was carefully packed into The Lift.

Endless lists were methodically checked off, as accumulated clothes and household items piled up at home. There were shoes and coats, underwear, dresses, blouses and skirts, suits and hats, topees to guard against the tropical sun. Family treasures like our silver candlesticks used on Friday nights, our menorah, family picture albums, personal papers, all were carefully packed. There were the wine goblets from the dining room which I had always loved, and my mother's Rosenthal china with the little roses on it. Also my doll carriage which I could not bear to part with, and my rather large doll collection.

Fortunately my mother had the foresight to secretly

separate my favorite doll called Maedi from the other dolls, and put her in our hand luggage. When she gave her to me once we were safely on the ship, I was overjoyed.

Edith and I were told to get our books and a few favorite toys and games together. We even packed rolls of toilet paper, soap, towels, blankets and sheets, because rumor had it that life in Shanghai was quite primitive. So here we were packing things we thought we absolutely could not live without. Radios, the kitchen icebox, crystal, canned goods, pillows, carpets, all earmarked for The Lift. Even my father's favorite brown leather arm chair, on which he always sat, while he had his breakfast. I used to rise early in the mornings, just so I could sit with him and get a bite of his buttered roll with cottage cheese and jam, before I got ready for school.

With an eye to keeping us intellectually stimulated, my father insisted that we carry our schoolbooks in our personal luggage. Edith and I would have preferred to pack them into The Lift instead. My father, of course, won that battle. As well as reading every day, we also had to study English, while on the ship sailing to Shanghai. Although he was not very fluent in the language, with the aid of his ever present dictionary, he taught us a few new words every day.

We had a little farewell party for our parakeet Kasimir, who exchanged his home on our kitchen window sill for one with a German family. They did not seem to mind that Kasimir was Jewish.

My mother's younger sister and her husband, Tante Liccie and Onkel Erwin, had decided to leave Germany with us. They also bribed the shipping officials and managed to get a cabin on the *Kashima Maru* with us.

The day we left Berlin, all six of us went to say good-bye

to my grandparents in Charlottenburg. My grandmother was still recuperating from her broken hip. The oldest daughter, my Tante Grete and her husband, decided to stay in Berlin and help my grandparents. Planning to wait a little longer before they would all try to join us in Shanghai, they were convinced that conditions for German Jews could not become worse than they already were. They still hoped that there would soon be a change for the better. As it turned out, this was only the beginning. Unfortunately, no amount of arguments from my parents would change their minds.

The last memory of my grandparents that is forever in my mind, is seeing them waving out of their window to us, as my mother and my aunt were crying and calling out to them. My mother refused to leave, so finally my father and my uncles had to carry her down the stairs, through the courtyard out to the street and into the taxi waiting to take us to *Anhalter Bahnhof*, (train station). Meanwhile, the German neighbors in the building who had known our family for years, watched from behind their lace curtains, not wanting to or daring to openly show any kindness or sympathy for Jews.

That day, my sister, then eleven years old, started to write her diary. She dedicated it to Omi who was supposed to read it on her arrival in Shanghai. But Omi and Opa, as well as Tante Grete and Onkel Martin never came.

12. KASHIMA MARU

The ocean liner, *Kashima Maru*, lay in the Naples harbor waiting to board her passengers. Most of these were refugees fleeing Nazi Germany, thankful to have gotten out with their lives and some of their possessions. Like us, they had bribed their way past eager officials to buy passage to what they hoped would be freedom, in many cases using money saved for a rainy day. They left behind them relatives and friends, their homes, and a way of life they were never to know again.

Our group included my parents, my sister and I, my Aunt Liccie and Uncle Erwin plus their parakeet Pippifax, who traveled comfortably in his cage under the hand-sown cover made by my aunt.

Departing Berlin by train, we stopped overnight in a hotel in Munich. Edith and I had our own room. We quickly got into mischief by pushing all the buttons on the wall and bringing the entire hotel staff to our door. My parents, not wanting to draw undue attention to our presence, did not appreciate this. We were severely reprimanded.

My father had a summons from the Gestapo in his pocket, ordering him to appear at their headquarters in Berlin, on May 19. By now it was May 18, and he was still not certain that he would be able to escape. He told me later, when I was much older, that he did not feel safe until we were actually on the ship, sailing away from Europe.

Another night was spent in Rome and one more in Naples, where my uncle Erwin insisted on ordering breakfast for all of us, with the aid of a German-Italian dictionary. None of us

41

got what we ordered, but aside from Edith and I, who thought this was all quite amusing, the adults seemed to have lost their appetite and their sense of humor all at the same time. It was May 21, 1939, when we finally boarded the *Kashima Maru*.

The ship's orchestra played, multicolored streamers thrown overboard by the passengers, fluttered in the wind. It all looked like a pleasure cruise on a luxury liner as we sailed away, except for the fact that many of the passengers were crying. The *Kashima Maru* was one of the ships of the *Nippon Yusen Kaisha Line*, registered in Tokyo, with a displacement of just under 10,000 tons. Not a large ship as ocean liners go, but we thought she was just the right size, with plenty of places to play hide and seek, or to conveniently be out of earshot, when our parents called us to gather for the daily English lesson.

My sister and I had our own cabin right next to our parents. We had bunkbeds, and took turns sleeping up on top or below. A washbowl built into the wall, slid out when needed. We were quite impressed and thought this was very cleverly done. We also looked forward to the hot saltwater baths located at the end of the gangway, for which appointments had to be made with the Japanese stewardess in charge of thick white towels.

We particularly liked to visit with members of the smiling, neatly outfitted Japanese crew, who always had some almond candy or tiny Japanese dolls to give us.

There were many children on board. All of us were constantly watched over by the kimono-clad stewardesses assigned to us. We all had our meals together in a separate dining room. Special events were arranged for us such as tea parties, for which we always wore our good taffeta party dresses. These parties were usually attended by the ship's

Captain and some of the crew. Ping-pong and shuffleboard tournaments were popular, as well as swim classes in the little pool on the back deck.

While we were having fun, we were aware, nevertheless, that our parents and the other adults were apprehensive about the future. They would sit on deck together and discuss at length how their lives had changed. The voyage was smooth except for a few severe typhoons (tropical cyclone). My mother suffered with seasickness and spent a lot of time lying down in her cabin. Whenever she felt better, she joined my father and the others up on deck.

The service in the first class was excellent and quite elegant for the grownups, with dancing and entertainment after dinner. The children's dinner was served before the adults, but we used to peek into the dining room windows to see what was going on, and whether my mother was saving any particularly tasty tidbits to give us later. There was one unfortunate little girl called Inge, whom we all teased a lot. She used to run howling loudly to her mother in the formal dining room, while the rest of us scattered and hid under the lifeboats. Edith and I looked upon the voyage as an unexpected extended holiday, we just enjoyed each day as a new adventure.

The *Kashima Maru* sailed through the Mediterranean, stopping briefly at Port Said, continued on through the Suez Canal, down the Red Sea to the port of Aden. We crossed the Arabian Sea docking in Bombay, India, then sailed down to Colombo on the Island of Ceylon, now called Sri Lanka, in the Indian Ocean. We continued on through the Strait of Malacca to Singapore, heading north along the coast of Indochina on the South China Sea, to Hongkong through the Strait of Formosa, before finally arriving in Shanghai. The voyage of the

Kashima Maru lasted thirty days. We had come more than halfway around the world.

We were only allowed off the ship at two ports. Controls for stateless persons were very tight. One thing I remember was going ashore in Bombay and buying icecream from a vendor on a crowded, noisy street. My parents felt sorry for a little beggar boy who had attached himself to us, and gave him some money. Another stop was made in Singapore, where we took a tour through the Botannical Gardens, a visit that was duplicated more than ten years later, when I passed through that part of the world again. That time though, I was running away from China, the very place I was headed for in 1939.

About six weeks after we left Berlin, the shipping company sent our Lift out on the ship *Nordmark*. A short time later war broke out. The *Nordmark* was detained in Singapore by British forces. Two years later we were contacted in Shanghai by Japanese authorities, who were then in power in Singapore. They planned to auction off the contents of the Lift, unless we paid them about One Thousand U.S. Dollars in storage fees. My father wrote to them that we did not have the money. We never found out what happened to our things. Everything connecting us to our past lives was gone.

13. SHANGHAI DAYS

The *Kashima Maru* docked right in the middle of the crowded Chinese section of town. After breathing fresh sea air for weeks, the smells of the harbor and the city assailed our somewhat delicate European noses. Oppressively humid summer heat, mixed with the smells of masses of sweating humanity who packed the dirty narrow streets, was quite different from the clean scrubbed atmosphere we had gotten used to on the *Kashima Maru*. Stepping ashore in Shanghai that summer in 1939, opened up a whole new world for us. We were met by sights, sounds and smells we had never even dreamed of.

There were so many people and so much noise everywhere. As far as the eye could see, there were always hundreds of people crowding the streets and shops. Many Chinese actually lived on the sidewalks in the summer, lying stretched out at night on straw mats in front of their hot airless shops, pedestrian traffic flowing on around them. They ate, drank, argued, and washed their children outdoors; tossing out the contents of washbasins and chamberpots, right into the gutters. In short, they set up housekeeping out on the sidewalks. People just walked around them as if it were nothing out of the ordinary. Instead, we were the ones who were out of the ordinary, and were stared at as if we had come from a different planet. We had landed in Hongkew, one of the most crowded areas in Shanghai. It was a long way from our carefully nurtured, sanitized existence in Berlin.

Chinese street vendors were busily hawking their wares.

Food of all kinds, clothing, piecegoods, live poultry and fish, all were carried in baskets hanging on opposite ends of a bamboo pole. This pole rested on the vendors' shoulders as they ran along the streets, shouting out their specialties. Some clicked pieces of bamboo in their hands, thus making a distinctive sound signaling whatever delicacy they were selling. Others chanted their wares in a loud sing-song voice.

The arrival of the man selling dried fruits and candies, known as *tucks*, or the popular tofu vendor, would always bring a crowd of eager buyers, many of them children clutching coins. Small cakes of soybean curd dipped in frying peanut oil were a treat to the natives, and later on to us, after we overcame our initial hesitation and parental warnings of ubiquitous germs.

The noodle vendor was another favorite. For a few pennies a bowl full of noodles and vegetables, with maybe a little meat or fish, could be bought. The vendor carried everything with him, including firewood and a large iron kettle used to boil the soup. Noisily his customers consumed their lunch as they squatted on their haunches.

Unforgettable was *Ta Ping Yu Sa Kwei* from the *Ta Ping* vendor. This consisted of a little pancake wrapped around a sort of twisted fried breadstick. Quite a delicacy, beloved by Chinese and foreigners alike.

There were fresh fish swimming in water tanks, next to their recently departed relatives, already pickled and salted in bottles. Strong odors emanated from meat and fowl hanging on hooks outside butcher shops.

Added to all this were heaps of decaying garbage in the streets that just about took our breath away. We were surprised to see little children relieving themselves right in the gutters. This was an old established custom. The children were dressed in pants that had open seams down the back, making toilet activities convenient for parent and child alike. It was a strange sight to us foreigners.

There was an abundance of noise everywhere. Chinese music blasted from shops, trolley cars made their way through jaywalking crowds with the drivers enthusiastically ringing their bells. Live chickens and ducks for sale in cages, added their cackling to the din. Drivers in automobiles honking their horns to get through the traffic, competed with the many bicycles and rickshaws on the street. Carts loaded sky high with merchandise for the markets, were pulled by a few sweating coolies, shouting at the crowds to make way.

Animated conversations were carried on between Chinese family members doing their daily shopping. Noisy bartering took place between shopkeepers and customers. By tradition the price of anything was negotiable. Bargaining was an expected and accepted way of life with Chinese merchants.

Everything seemed to happen right out on the sidewalk. There was the barber with his little stool for the customer, his comb and scissors ready at a moments notice. Wizened old women, loudly scolding, would try to catch up with their little grandchildren. Some of the old ladies leaned heavily on canes, their tiny feet bound, according to ancient Chinese custom. A practice long since outlawed. Fortune tellers who not only read fortunes for a few pennies, but also told ancient fairy tales and wrote letters for the illiterate, sat on little bamboo chairs. They were surrounded by an appreciative audience, busily spitting sunflower seeds onto the sidewalk. Old men sat in front of tea houses, noisily slurping their tea from little bowls, as they played mah jongg. They, in turn, were watched and given advice on their next move, by interested bystanders.

Edith and I were fascinated by all the new sights and sounds, as our rickshaw coolies ran along, pulling us through the crowded streets to our new home. Beggars carrying babies in their arms ran beside us. During all our years in China we never got used to the beggars. Some of them were dirty little children with open sores, begging for food: "*Mipoh, Mipoh*," (give me bread).

Whenever we tried to ignore them, the braver ones cursed at us: "*Nakoning Pissae*." Loosely translated that meant, that foreigners were pigs.

Friends welcoming us at the dock, took us to rooms they had rented for us in the Wayside district.

"Safety in numbers," my father remarked, "we'll stay where there are other people like us."

My mother was too overcome by the heat and the crowds of people around, to say anything. She was just relieved to be on dry land again, after being seasick for so long.

Hongkew was an area where most of the European refugees settled, when they first arrived. Housing was affordable there for those, who had managed to bring out even a little money from Germany. Others who were financially better off or who had friends or relatives who preceded them, very quickly moved to the International Settlement or French Concession areas of Shanghai. Conditions there were much better and more comfortable. In fact, it was often comparable to the standard of living left behind in Europe.

For the thousands of refugees who could not find or afford to pay for rooms, relief organizations had set up settlement camps known by the German word *Heime*, where they could live. Also there were soup kitchens, a school and a hospital staffed with refugee doctors and nurses, available for the new arrivals. The organizations, funded by multi-national local philanthropists, as well as by American contributions, played an integral part in helping thousands of displaced persons become situated in their new surroundings.

I remember eating my first meal in Shanghai in the Ward Road *Heim*, one of the largest of the settlement camps, on the day we arrived. We sat on wooden benches in a large room together with other people from our ship. They fed us string beans with meat and potatoes. We liked it. No one had any complaints.

The first few weeks we ate all our meals there. In the beginning, Edith and I ate in the children's kitchen, where there was always an extra ration of boiled milk, and often, even our favorite farina cereal. Later on, we picked up the food once a day, in stacked metal containers bought at a Chinese shop, and brought it home to eat. When eventually we moved to a house where there was a kitchen, my mother and my aunt cooked our meals at home.

Hostilities between Chinese and Japanese factions in 1937, resulted in the leveling and partial destruction of many areas in Hongkew. Two years later, when we arrived, there were still many houses in ruins and piles of rubble in the streets. Hongkew used to be an industrial area, it was not known as one of the more picturesque areas of Shanghai. The pervasive look of poverty and decay, made it appear even less inviting.

Our new home, in a lane on Seward Road, consisted of one large room for our family of four. My uncle and aunt had a smaller room in the same house. Owned by German refugees, the house consisted of nine rooms, each inhabited by a family. There was a straw rug on the floor, several couches for sitting and sleeping, a table and some chairs and a wardrobe. Kitchen facilities were not available except for a primitive Chinese kitchen downstairs, which was ruled over by the owner's servants. The bathroom consisted of two large covered buckets used as toilets, a wash basin and a shower. A second shower was located upstairs on the roof garden.

Every morning, while we all held our noses, the man with the "honeycart," came to carry away the contents of the buckets used by inhabitants of the house. This in turn became fertilizer on fields in the nearby countryside, where vegetables were grown.

It took some time to get used to the weather in Shanghai. Summer temperatures were much higher than any we had ever experienced. There was so much humidity in the air, that our clothes and shoes quickly became damp and moldy. We tried to keep ourselves clean as best as we could, but with very limited bathroom facilities, sanitation was always a problem. Prickly heat and skin infections were common.

By contrast, the winters were severely cold. In spite of the warm clothing we brought from Germany, it was not unusual for us to have chilblains on our fingers and toes during the damp winter weather.

14. MACKA-LECKA-LU

The city of Shanghai was divided into several different sections. Hongkew, our asylum, was located in an area north of Soochow Creek. It was also known locally as the Wayside District. Poorer class Chinese natives lived there in large numbers. As the area became more and more overcrowded, their huts and makeshift hovels spread out for miles beyond Hongkew.

Crossing over Soochow Creek by way of Garden Bridge, you would find yourself on the Bund. This was a large avenue facing the bustling waterfront, that was part of the larger expanse of the International Settlement, controlled by foreign authorities. The Settlement was, to a large extent, inhabited by foreigners. These were American and British nationals, also Russians, Germans and citizens of other European countries, as well as wealthy upper-class Chinese, who often lived in magnificent homes. The center of commerce was established on the Bund. The old maritime companies had their headquarters there, as did many of the foreign banks, newspaper offices and the consulates of many foreign countries. Their massive stone buildings were part of the Shanghai skyline.

Ships sailing under many different flags, as well as Chinese vessels, docked in the harbor in front of the Bund. Hundreds of Chinese junks used as houseboats, crowded the malodorous Whangpoo River. Whole families lived their entire lives on these boats.

I remember the sound of the chimes of Big Ben on the Customs House clock tower, overlooking the busy harbor. The sound of bells ringing out from above, always brings back memories of the Shanghai Bund to me.

Paradoxically, you would find large private estates surrounded by high walls, adjacent to very poor sections, where natives lived in overcrowded shacks. Smartly uniformed Chinese or Sikh watchmen, whose job it was to guard office buildings, public areas or private homes, spent much of their time chasing beggars away from the entrances.

A large contingent of White Russians, refugees of the Bolshevik revolution, had also settled in Shanghai since the early 1920's, making up a sizeable part of the foreign population.

The streets of the International Settlement were full of well stocked shops of every description, selling some of the finest artifacts, silks and satins of the Orient. There were foreign and Chinese department stores, restaurants and dance halls, and everywhere there were people. Day or night, the streets were always full of people, walking or riding the buses, taxicabs, bicycles or rickshaws; intent on their daily business.

You could hire a rickshaw and travel down crowded Nanking Road, past the Foreign Y.M.C.A. and the Park Hotel, to the Race Course, where horse racing was a favorite pastime, along with sports events sponsored by many different clubs in the city. The Race Course was one of the major recreational and social centers used by foreigners in Shanghai, except during the war years, when the Japanese took it over for military use.

The French Concession, another foreign enclave within Shanghai, was a large picturesque area with beautiful tree lined streets, churches, parks and apartment buildings. Many French nationals and other well-to-do foreigners made their home there. Partially due to the civilized aspect of this section, the city of Shanghai was sometimes referred to as the Paris of the East. Looking at the fashionable shops, many fine restaurants and sidewalk cafes, private clubs with recreational facilities and schools of different nationalities, aside from the presence of rickshaws and pedicabs, it looked almost like any modern European city.

Beyond Bubbling Well Road lay the Western District. This was not as densely populated as the other areas. Situated on the outskirts of Shanghai, a quieter atmosphere prevailed here. St. John's University and Jessfield Park, with its beautifully landscaped gardens, were well-known landmarks of the Western District. It was also the home of choice of many wealthy foreigners, living in luxurious villas surrounded by large private gardens. Their every wish was quickly attended to by Chinese servants, known as amahs and boys, who were sometimes called by number, corresponding to their importance or authority in the household.

Growing up in Shanghai, most of my time was spent in Hongkew, the place of our arrival. It was only when I started to attend the Seymour Road School, a few years later, that I went back and forth every day by tramcar. The route was up Wayside Road, crossing over the Garden Bridge, riding along the Bund and then down Nanking Road into Bubbling Well and Carter Roads, eventually arriving at school nearly an hour later.

Our first year in Shanghai, saw us move out of the single room that was our first home. My father and my uncle took over the management of a large house on Ford Lane. We all moved in there together, still accompanied by my aunt's by now aging Pippifax.

While my parents had their own problems with the tenants in this new house, some of whom would not or could not pay the rent, Edith and I were delighted with our new surroundings. Here we were in this huge white stuccoed house surrounded by a high fence, with all the freedom we wanted. We could run and play around the house and garden, but we were not permitted to go outside the gates to the street by ourselves.

Again we shared a bedroom together. In later years Edith told me of a nightmare she often had, when sleeping in that room with me. It was of a man carrying a rucksack, who was passing by the window. My memories are also of that bedroom. I pictured it as having a secret door, that lead to another room with high barred windows. Edith insisted, however, that no such room ever existed. So maybe it was also a dream.

There was a large enclosed garden, where many trees and flowers grew, just perfect for playing games with the other children, who lived in the house. Through the black iron fence we looked out on the busy street beyond, teeming with Chinese, while all was quiet and peaceful in the garden.

My mother and my aunt, with their knitting baskets, used to sit together in the sun out on the stone patio. Meanwhile, through the french doors leading to our spacious kitchen, you could detect something fragrant, bubbling on the stove inside. Both of them were skilled at knitting and crocheting. They knitted sweaters to sell as piecework. White sweaters with colored threads running through, punctuated by little raised circles that we called *Noppen*, in German.

Edith, who was also handy with a knitting needle, got to knit some of the smaller pieces for them. I had no such talents and used up the left over wool to make somewhat distorted potholders. They were usually short at one end, and long on the other.

Within a year, my parents, uncle and aunt, realized that their rental management of the house on Ford Lane proved to be a financially unstable enterprise. Reluctantly, we packed our things and all of us moved to MacGregor Road, into several rented rooms.

When the tram conductor called out: "*Macka-Lecka-Lu*" in pidgin English, we used to gather our schoolbags, jump off the tram and run down the street towards home.

I liked it there in the old stone house covered with ivy. Besides us, several other refugee families lived there also. My parents, Edith and I had two large rooms with a verandah, in the front of the house. The kitchen and bathroom were shared with the other tenants. In spite of some squabbling that went on, regarding allotted time of the facilities, on the whole it worked out fairly well. Living conditions were quite adequate, for refugee standards at least, and certainly better than the way many other people had to live.

In front of our verandah, there was a long narrow garden full of clothes lines propped up with bamboo poles, and waving poplar trees reaching high into the sky. The garden was enclosed by stone walls; a padlocked gate led out to the street. I used to climb over the garden wall and visit the people in the house next-door. They had brought many German children's books with them, which they let me borrow. Among my favorites was the *Nesthaekchen* series, a story about the youngest child of a family, living in Germany. Each successive book described her adventures until she married, went to South America with her husband and had children of her own.

I loved all thirteen volumes of this popular series. I used to sit in the garden under the shady trees, with the current house cat on my lap, and read them over and over. Not yet quite comfortable with the English language, I was perfectly happy with these German stories. At that time I was still translating from German to English in my head, before I spoke. It was only later when I became truly bilingual, that the translations ceased, and eventually I even dreamed in English. To this day though, when I look at a dictionary, in my mind I run through the alphabet in German instead of English.

On hot summer evenings, all the occupants of 69 MacGregor Road, came out into the garden carrying their chairs, their lemonade and their smoky mosquito coils to chase away the mosquitoes. My mother and my aunt always brought some handwork out with them. Everyone sat in a circle on the grass, as the evening hours passed and the stars came out. The grownups talked about the old days and the new. The men compared notes about their ventures into the Shanghai business world. My father and my uncle went to the city every day to find jobs. Eventually my father found work in the office of a Chemical Company. It was all quite unfamiliar to him, he had to learn everything from the bottom up. To make it even harder, the official language was English, with which he still had some trouble. But at least it was a job and we had an income. Even though his salary was quite small, my parents were very frugal and knew how to manage money. We lived very simply, without any luxuries. Still, I don't ever remember going hungry during those years, or at any other time either.

There was usually some shuffling about for the best

position, those humid nights in the garden. Frau Markus, our landlady, did not want to sit next to Frau Blum, not one of her favorite tenants. In her opinion: "She is too conceited, always acting like a princess."

Some of the ladies did not mind at all sitting near Herr Probst, who was tall and handsome and knew how to tell a story. As we used to do on the ship, my sister and I still enjoyed chasing his daughter Inge around. She always dutifully cooperated by screaming and disrupting ongoing conversations. When we got older and a little bit smarter, we eventually became good friends with her. Of course, nobody wanted to get near little Guenther, the young son of one of the tenants. He always had a runny nose and whined a lot.

Children were allowed to stay up past their bedtime to catch the evening breezes. We all tried to sit next to our Onkel Erwin, who enjoyed telling us jokes and performing his old magic tricks for us. Somehow, it never got boring, no matter how often he made his thumb disappear, only to produce it again from his vest pocket. "*Ach*, Erwin, you're not going to do that again?" my Tante Liccie would murmur resignedly, rolling her eyes.

My father often took pictures of us, on the steps of the house on MacGregor Road. I still have them in my photo album. All of us lined up according to height or age, or whatever he thought would look good.

Permanently captured on film, are my Onkel Erwin and Tante Liccie, my parents, Edith and I. My sister and I are wearing our good navy blue dresses with the red taffeta ties, a farewell present from my father's boss at the stationery firm in Berlin. We all stand there with our arms linked, smiling broadly, even though our shoes had gotten too tight since we brought them from Germany. My mother and my aunt in their hand-knitted dresses, their hair severely pulled back in the fashion of the day, looking younger and somehow quite vulnerable to me today. Next to them is my uncle, attired as always with a bow tie and wearing his funny round spectacles. Then of course, there is my father, natty in his three piece suit, slightly breathless from running to take his place while the camera was set on a timer.

15. REQUIEM FOR RUTH

M ost afternoons, after school, we listened to Radio Station XMHA. During the Children's Hour, which always started off with *The Teddy Bear's Picnic* theme song, my best friend Ruth Katz and I used to dedicate songs to each other. Not having access to a telephone, we wrote letters to Auntie Peggy, the lady in charge of the program, and asked her to send a song to Rose from Carnation, or the other way around. I don't remember which one of us was Rose and which one was Carnation, but we thought these names were much more exotic than our real ones. We made a pact that we would never tell anyone who we really were.

We always went to school together, and I did not think there was anything unusual in Ruth's habit of stooping down every few steps and touching the street with her hand. It slowed us down a bit, but she said it made her feel good to do it and I should try it sometime. I never felt the need, so I would just wait for her to get it over with and go on walking.

Some winter mornings, a gruesome sight would greet us on the way to school. Beggars who froze to death overnight, were lying in the street. Often, particularly in the poorer neighborhoods, little wrapped up bundles, containing frozen babies, would be out on the curb, waiting to be picked up by the sanitation carts. Poor Chinese families with too many children, often put their newborn babies, mainly the females, out to die. They tried to keep their sons alive to carry on the family tradition, while daughters were considered just another mouth to feed, according to the old way of Chinese thinking.

Our family backgrounds were similar. Ruth arrived in

Shanghai from Germany with her parents, around the same time that we did. Her parents tried to make a living by running a small cafe in a little courtyard in front of their home. Ruth was their only child. They absolutely doted on her. With her light brown hair and blue eyes, Rutchen, as they lovingly called her, could do no wrong.

One hot summer day we were both invited by one of the American Relief Agencies to go on a picnic. We were ecstatic. Now we could see for ourselves, what the other children had boasted about. A big park where there were meadows, trees and flowers. We would have lots of fun and games and best of all, cakes, candies and lemonade supplied by the Agency.

Together we climbed onto an open truck, already packed with our schoolmates, for the long ride through the city streets. Our mothers' instructions to hold on to the sides of the truck, so we would not fall off, ringing in our ears.

We had a wonderful time at the park, delighted to get away from our crowded homes and the hot smelly streets of Hongkew for a day. When we came home that evening, tired, sunburned, but very contented, our parents were waiting for us. We could not stop telling them about our exciting day. A few hours later Ruth collapsed, and shortly afterward died of heat exhaustion.

I was inconsolable. It was my first personal experience with death. My parents did not want me to attend her funeral. They thought that at twelve years of age, I was too young. However, I was determined to go, and I sneaked out of the house. From the Chinese flower seller on the corner, I bought a bunch of roses and carnations, and made my way to the cemetery.

Funerals in Shanghai were very simple then. There was

already a gas shortage. The coffin, more often than not, was transported to the cemetery by bicycle cart. According to Jewish custom, burial took place before sundown of the next day.

I remember the endless tram ride out to the cemetery. It was several miles outside Hongkew. I sat there holding onto my flowers, looking out of the window at the unfamiliar streets. There were other mourners on the tram. One of them was our Hebrew teacher, whom Ruth and I were not fond of. I think I actually hated her, when she took a mirror out of her purse and fixed her hair, which was flying around in the hot, dusty wind.

"She has no heart! How can she think of her looks at a time like this?" I asked myself unhappily.

Gently I laid the flowers on the simple closed coffin. Ruth's mother kept touching me. Crying loudly, she begged me to tell her where her Rutchen had gone. I had no answers.

My roses and carnations were the only flowers there. This seemed a little odd to me. It was not until later, that I learned it was not customary to bring flowers to a Jewish funeral. But I always felt that Ruth would have understood.

That day marked the end of my childhood years. It was time to grow up. No more lazy days in the garden with Ruth. No more playing of games and making believe we were fairy tale princesses with flowery names. No more thoughts of returning to Berlin to the old life, and picking up where we left off. Everything was changing with terrifying speed.

16. AN ENGLISHMAN ON A BICYCLE

Shortly after our arrival in Shanghai, my sister and I were enrolled in a school called the Shanghai Jewish Youth Association. The school's chief benefactor was a wealthy, somewhat eccentric Englishman named Sir Horace Kadoorie. He was a member of a well-known Sephardic family, recognized for their many philanthropic activities in the Far East. He built this school in the Hongkew district exclusively for refugee children arriving from Europe. It was soon filled to overflowing.

A welcome interruption of the school routine would occur on the days, when he arrived for one of his frequent inspections. Children and teachers put their books in order, spruced up the classrooms and wiped down the dusty blackboards with a sponge. We all practiced phrases in our newly learned English, just in case we were lucky enough to be asked a question by Sir Horace or some of his entourage.

It just so happened that Sir Horace once said something to me during these visits, but neither of us understood what the other one said. He smiled, patted me on the head and moved on, as I beamed from ear to ear. The rest of that day, I was the center of attraction on the playground. "What did he say, how did it feel? He actually touched you!"

Our head mistress, Mrs. Hartwich, had us all line up in front of the U-shaped school building and give three cheers for Sir Horace, when he got ready to leave.

"Hip Hip Hurrah", we all yelled with great abandon, as he rode around on his bicycle, wearing white shorts and a white shirt, his topee on his head shielding him against the hot sun.

It was always very exciting for us. What an interesting way to spend the morning and what a sight it was for our unsophisticated eyes. Here was a real live Englishman on a bicycle. We could not wait to go home and share the story with our parents.

Our teachers at the S.J.Y.A. or Kadoorie School, as it was generally called, consisted of some refugee teachers, but mostly the teaching staff was British. They spoke nothing but English, the children spoke only German. This problem was overcome in a surprisingly short time. The teachers taught us to sing songs almost totally by rote.

Enthusiastically we sang songs like: *Clementine* and *My Bonnie Lies over the Ocean,* or *It's a Long Way to Tipperary.* At first, most of us had no idea what we were singing, making up in volume, by what we lacked in understanding. But in a short time we learned to speak, read and write in English.

During recess in the hot summer months, we lined up on the playground for tea, dipping our cups into large buckets, containing lukewarm sweetened tea. Sometimes, when the water was not boiled long enough, we got stomach aches. There were so many germs everywhere, that all our drinking water was always boiled. At home all the fresh fruit and vegetables that we ate, were first washed in a solution of potassium permanganate, then rinsed with boiled water. I often volunteered for this job because I liked the purple color of the potassium.

17. SCHOOL DAYS

The first year or so that we were in Shanghai, I was reluctant to read English books, because I found them too difficult. Faithfully I read and re-read my old German story books. Once I even wrote a little story in German of which I was very proud. It was entitled "Tessa in the Swiss Alps."

Well, unfortunately my sister found it, tucked away in my underwear drawer. She read it out loud together with her girlfriend Eva. Both promptly dissolved into fits of laughter. It was not supposed to be a comedy. I was highly insulted and complained tearfully to my mother about this invasion of my privacy. After that experience, I hid my writings in a different place.

My father kept taking me to the little library in the neighborhood. He tried very hard to introduce me to the books on the English shelf. Finally one day just to please him, I took a story about girls living in boarding schools in England. That turned the tide. From then on I read only in English. I absolutely loved those stories.

Often I daydreamed that I was a rich English schoolgirl, with long blond hair; the possessor of a fair complexion without even one single freckle. I would be dressed in an immaculate school uniform that never wrinkled, going home on school holidays to a mansion equipped with a Mummy, a Daddy, a butler, maids and gardeners. All of this, of course, while speaking perfect English, without a trace of German accent. I dreamed of a life I had never seen. A life totally removed from my own refugee existence, where I was struggling to adapt to so many new things.

Sometimes, after we came home from school, we went to Wayside Park to play on the swings and the see-saws. But the biggest thrill for us was, when we were chosen by one of the relief agencies to go on a real picnic to Jessfield Park. We all crowded together on the large open trucks that picked us up, standing up during the whole ride, laughing and singing newly learned English songs. My mother was always very nervous when we went off on the trucks. Our packed lunch of sandwiches, cookies and soda supplied by the committee, was another treat. We were not used to luxuries at home, so these little extra things were always much appreciated.

Jessfield Park was a large park also containing a zoo, on the western side of Shanghai, adjacent to St. John's University. Beautifully landscaped with many trees and flowers it was like an oasis to us, coming out of the dreary Hongkew district. We stared at all the well dressed people. All of us agreed, that they must be very rich to have the time just to wander around, and even pay money for the entrance ticket.

In time, my sister and I were transferred to the Shanghai Jewish School on Seymour Road, even though it would mean some financial hardship for my parents to pay the school fees. We were put on the waiting list. Children living in the International Settlement and in the French Concession, (or in "The French" as we called it at home) had precedence over refugee children coming out of Hongkew. It was quite some time before we were actually admitted to the Seymour Road School, with my sister getting in a year before I did.

My parents paid Five Dollars per month tuition fees for us. We were instructed daily to do our best, to make the expense worth while.

This school was known for its high academic standard and

was run in the British tradition. The headmaster and teachers were kind, but strict. Discipline and proper behavior by the students was absolutely mandatory. After-school detentions were freely given out for even minor infractions of the rules.

Scholastically the school was superior to the S.J.Y.A. There we often rehearsed at great length for theatrical productions, while happily neglecting our schoolwork. Once, to my delight, I was picked to play *Gretel* in a *Hansel and Gretel* production. I dressed up in my *dirndl* dress brought along from Germany, liberally applied my mother's lipstick and rouge to my face and did my interpretation of *Gretel* on the stage. Forgetting my habitual shyness, I even performed a song and dance routine with a rather reluctant *Hansel*. Enjoying myself thoroughly, I was sure that I was destined to be an actress.

Aside from some of the more formidable teachers in the new school, the person who truly terrified most of us was Mr. Ying, the school secretary. A Chinese gentleman of indeterminate age, always neat and trim, with a pencil thin moustache over an unsmiling mouth, who, when not in his office haughtily dispensing books and papers, could be seen patrolling the halls dressed in his long grey Chinese gown. Unerringly, he descended on us, if we loitered by the water fountain, or took the long way around to go to the lavatory during class. He did not miss much. It seemed that his eyes and ears were everywhere. Little time was wasted by him reporting unwary students, who tried to bend the rules a little.

Many nationalities were represented at the school on Seymour Road. As Hongkew refugees, we felt properly intimidated at first by so many different children, who took their time making friends with us and often made fun of our

German accents. The girls' serge school uniforms were always perfectly pressed, all the pleats in their skirts hung razor straight. I, on the other hand, usually felt somewhat untidy in my blue cotton tunic that tended to look crushed, as soon as I sat down.

Coming in from Hongkew after an hour long streetcar ride, I was always hungry. I often got demerits for raising my desk and sampling the sandwich my mother had packed for me, instead of waiting for the recess bell to ring. I was still rather timid in those days and did not like to assert myself. That did not work out too well for me one day, when after running races in the hot sun during gym class, I let myself be pushed back from the water fountain by my equally thirsty classmates. They, together with hastily summoned school officials, finally took notice of me after I passed out from the heat and landed on the floor in a dead faint.

18.   YOU TAKE HER

At a fairly early age, it became apparent to me, that athletics was not a favorite subject on my curriculum. I was quite happy to just run around and play games with my friends on a noncompetitive basis, but any organized sport activity was definitely on the list of things I tried to avoid.

Even during my early school days in Germany, I already had experiences that pointed to questionable talents in that direction, not to mention a lack of confidence and skills. Take for instance, the Berlin Macabee Sports Club fiasco, of which I can still hear echoes in my head.

Our whole family had joined the club on my mother's behest, she being very keen on physical culture and healthful habits for all of us. My father and I did our best to keep up at the different gym classes, where the instructors tried, more often than not unsuccessfully, to teach us to climb ropes or run obstacle races, but we were definitely no match for my mother and my sister. Both of them enjoyed sports and were good at it, catching a ball, when it was thrown to them during games and tossing it in fine form on to someone else. Not so my father and I, whose hands dropped many a ball and lost many a game for the team we were on.

My mother was always a good athlete and had been a swimming champion in her youth. Edith following in her footsteps, was also a very enthusiastic player at all kinds of games. She eventually became a ping-pong champion in Shanghai, when she was in her teens.

It was my father and I, who did not always measure up in this category. Well, I consoled myself, at least I was in good company.

Once, the childrens class I was enrolled in, worked on the apparatus in the Macabee gymnasium. I remember falling off the horse like a stone and hitting my head on the floor. There was a loud bang at which point all activity in the gym ceased for a moment. I had really brought things to a standstill this time, and my head hurt for quite a while afterwards. But at least it got me out of gym class, as my mother finally decided, that maybe this was not so healthy for me.

Both Edith and I learned to swim at Wannsee Lake near Berlin, my mother and my aunts teaching us the breast stroke during summer vacations. I did my own lopsided version of this stroke, always taking care to keep my face out of the water.

My so-called expertise did not prevent me from nearly drowning in the *Kashima Maru* swimming pool, on our way to Shanghai. An enthusiastic passenger called Karola, who liked to practice her skills at lifesaving, grabbed me by the neck as I was paddling around one day just having a good time. As she tried to pull me to the end of the pool to show off how well she could do this, I panicked and went under. The more I struggled, the more water I swallowed, especially when I could no longer feel the bottom of the pool under my feet.

My mother, sitting in her deck chair, swiftly came to the rescue. She jumped into the pool fully clothed and pulled me out crying, coughing and spitting. Then she turned around and gave my would-be savior a smack in the face and a tongue-lashing that could be heard all over the ship.

For all the years we lived in Shanghai afterwards, whenever we met Karola on the street, she would cross over to the other side and pretend not to see us.

I was a fairly average student during my school years in Shanghai. My favorite subjects were English, history and composition, which I enjoyed, but mathematics was a struggle from start to finish. I always had the feeling that I needed just a little more time and attention in order to know what I was doing. As it was, I often found myself wandering around in a maze of numbers, not quite able to figure out where I was going. I liked music and art and did quite well in Hebrew and Bible studies that were taught in the Jewish schools I attended. We also studied Chinese, and later on during the war, Japanese was added to our curriculum, by order of the Japanese authorities.

With the exception of field hockey, an activity I enjoyed, sports in general remained my nemesis all during my school years. On the playing field, I once briefly distinguished myself by swinging my hockey stick at the wrong angle, thereby hitting the girl behind me and sending her to the hospital with a fractured jaw. During recess, or even in gym class, I was usually the last one to be picked for games. "You take her!" "No, you take her!" the leaders of the teams would yell at one another as I, embarrassed and beet-red down to my toes, would murmur that I did not really want to play anyway.

Little did I know in those dreadful moments, that in a few short years I would transcend all this misery. That I would wind up giving out sport trophies at the school's assemblies, as the bride of one of the most popular sport teachers the school had ever had.

19. FIFTY ONE CHUSAN ROAD

Stateless Refugees Are Prohibited To Pass Here Without Permission. Suddenly the signs appeared; prominently posted in Hongkew by the Japanese Army, all along the boundaries of the segregated area. Already we were required, at all times, to carry our Resident Certificate with us. These certificates with our pictures on it, also had a yellow line across the top that plainly identified us as Jewish refugees. In addition, we now had to obtain permission from the Japanese, to travel in and out of the designated area. As of May 1943, Jewish refugees wishing to leave the district to go to school or work in the International Settlement or Frenchtown (colloquial for French Concession), were required to obtain a special passport from the Japanese Commander, Mr. Ghoya. After obtaining this pass, we had to wear a little metal badge in a visible spot on our clothing, on which the words "May Pass" were printed in Chinese.

The internment of stateless refugees began in Shanghai, a little over a year after the Japanese bombed Pearl Harbor in December of 1941. The Japanese Military Command decreed that the roughly 20,000 refugees who had fled from Europe to Shanghai arriving there after 1937, were to move into a designated area in Hongkew, measuring about one mile by two and a half miles. Those arriving before the year 1937 were not affected by this order.

The area was already crowded with European refugees and Chinese living side by side. Several of the settlement camps, as well as the Ward Road Hospital staffed by refugees, were located there. Situated in the poorer section of

Hongkew, with many of the ruins of the Japanese bombardment in the late thirties still visible, the sudden influx of thousands of people turned it into an even more crowded, unsanitary and inhospitable place. The deadline for moving into this designated area, also referred to as a ghetto, or often simply as "The District," was May, 1943.

This edict precipitated a hectic scramble to find a place to live within that section. At the time of the proclamation, our family still lived in the house on MacGregor Road. As this was situated outside the area designated by the Japanese, we had to move. Our landlord, himself a German refugee, exchanged the house on MacGregor Road, with one located inside the district. Many of his tenants moved with him to the new house.

We considered ourselves lucky to rent one room on the second floor of 51 Chusan Road. We were right in the center of the designated area. My uncle and aunt also moved next door to us into a tiny, dark room in the same house.

Headquarters For The Bureau For Stateless Refugees, was located on Muirhead Road, inside the designated area. Proof in the form of signed documents by schools or businesses, ascertaining that the refugees had a valid reason for leaving the district, had to be presented to Mr. Ghoya. He then handed out the necessary passport to us - if he felt so inclined.

This special passport from the Japanese Military had to be shown to any Japanese soldier or Pao Chia member, stationed around the segregated area, who asked for it. The Foreign Pao Chia was made up of refugees required to act as a compulsory self-governing police force, under strict control of the Japanese Military Forces.

Mr. Ghoya, the Japanese Commander, was a small

statured man, who often stood on his desk to make himself taller. He liked to refer to himself as "King of the Jews." We used to line up for hours on the street outside his office every few weeks, to have our pass renewed. While he was often nice to children and sometimes even gave us candy, when we answered questions to his satisfaction and were deferential enough to suit him, he nevertheless had a very bad temper so that you never quite knew what to expect. If he was in a good mood, things went smoothly. More often than not, he was in a foul temper and amused himself with lengthy, shouted questioning of the applicants. Making them go back to the end of the line, or slapping the men around and throwing cold water over them, was not unusual behavior for him. Once in a while, he liked to lock people up in jail for a day or two for no reason. This was potentially very dangerous because all kinds of communicable diseases were rampant in the crowded, filthy cells.

Sometimes in a fit of rage, Mr. Ghoya refused to give out passes altogether. For the adults this had a disastrous effect, as they were now unable to get to their jobs in the city. With so many people already trying to make a living, earning any money inside the district became harder and harder as time went on.

It was always a terrifying experience for us to get our passes to go to school, even though we usually went with my father, who also needed permission to go to his office job in Shanghai.

Looking back today, I think my father was probably just as scared as we were, but he seemed a tower of strength to us then. My uncle and my aunt both worked in offices outside the ghetto and also went through the same experience. My aunt always had a headache afterwards, and would have to lie down with a cold compress on her head. My mother never left the ghetto during those years, but stayed home and kept house for us. She was always anxious until we were all safely home again every day, within the time limit stamped on our passes.

Our new home was in a house three stories high, with about four or five rooms on each floor. Each room contained an entire family and their belongings. We had to sell or leave behind some of our things, so that we could all fit into such a cramped space. One corner of our room was used as a kitchen. It had a small sink with running cold water, and a gas burner which we rarely used because gas was strictly rationed. My mother learned to cook on a native charcoal burner set on the windowsill. This not only gave off lots of smoke but also kept going out. We took turns fanning the flame with a bamboo fan.

My parents bought staples such as rice, sugar and flour by the sack, often on the black market, when food was unavailable in the shops. There were always a lot of bugs in these sacks. My mother would first let us pick out the weevils from the rice. This sometimes turned into a race between my sister and I, to see who got the highest body count. Mutti then washed the picked over rice and let it come to a boil. Quickly she wrapped up the pot in old newspapers, put it in the middle of one of the beds and covered it with blankets. The result was perfectly steamed rice every time.

Of course if one of us wanted to take a nap, we were stopped by someone yelling: "Don't lie down there, the rice is in the bed." For years I thought that everyone cooked rice that way.

Our communal bathroom was at the end of a dark corridor. It served the sixteen people who lived on our floor. There were also large numbers of insects of all kinds. They had established residence in the bathroom long before the refugees moved in. I was especially frighted of the large flying cockroaches who dive-bombed us at the most inopportune times. We used this room only, when absolutely necessary.

Actually there was another bathroom for the dozen or so people living on the top floor. This one had a window, which made it a little better than ours on the second floor, which had none. In spite of that very favorable point, and even though there was occasionally toilet paper up there, instead of the torn up newspapers we were using downstairs, my parents discouraged us from using it. It was right next-door to the room where "Those Women" lived.

Two sisters from Germany lived there with their husbands. While the men were out trying to make a living, the two women did the same at home by entertaining Japanese officers in their room. We could hear a lot of shrieking and laughing, and the sound of heavy army boots being dropped on the floor. Some time later, the by now rather tipsy officers would stagger down the stairs, yelling "*Sayonara*," and waving to the sisters, who stood giggling on the landing, wearing their Japanese silk kimonos. The two of them always seemed to have money, plenty of food and nice clothes.

"I'll explain it to you when you get older. In the meantime you are not allowed to talk to them." My mother belonged to a generation that did not believe in sex education.

We were taught to sponge-bathe ourselves, usually with cold water, in our little kitchen corner. Behind a curtain hung up for privacy, we splashed around as best as we could. We washed ourselves in three sections, drying and dressing each portion before starting on the next one. The first part was up to the waist, the second part went up to the knees and then we put our feet in the basin to be washed last. About once a week, we washed each other's hair with water heated on the stove. Upon the sound of approaching footsteps during these watery maneuvers, we sounded the alarm: "Stay out, I'm taking a bath."

My parents slept on two couches at one end of the room. During the day their bedding was tucked into drawers under the couch. My sister and I slept on army cots near the two windows.

Every two weeks or so, especially in the summer when the itching became unbearable, we made war on the bedbugs. We bought boiling hot water from the water seller out in the street. Hurrying home before the water cooled, we poured it along the seams and creases of the couches and the cots. After that dried out, we removed the dead bedbugs from the beds. On Sunday afternoons it passed as a family group activity.

Piled one on top of the other, against the wall, covered with a tablecloth, our old steamer trunks from Germany were used to store our things. In the middle of the room there was a table and several chairs used for meals, conversation, home-work and sewing. My mother always managed to have fresh flowers on the table. Also close at hand, were several flyswat-ters ready for any unwelcome guests, flying in through the un-screened windows. We had a lot of books in the room, and one old radio. Occasionally we managed to tune into *The Voice of America*. It was usually jammed, and as it was on the list of forbidden things, as far as the Japanese were concerned, we did not take too many chances on getting caught. Mostly we listened to local radio stations, which gave censored news about the war and also played an abundance of classical and popular music.

"And one, two, three, and one, two, three, and turn," to the strains of Vienna waltzes on the radio, my father taught me to dance in that crowded room. Usually my mother sang along, and Edith watched critically from the sidelines awaiting her turn.

20. OUR PIECE OF AMERICA

During the latter part of the war, many air raids were carried out by United States bombers, from bases in Okinawa and the interior of China. The American Air Force attempted to knock out utility companies and Japanese military installations along the Shanghai waterfront.

Later we found out, that they tried to avoid civilian areas, but unfortunately they were not always successful. Certainly there was damage to Japanese military units, but there was also damage to the civilian population. The segregated area, with its thousands of refugees was located very near the waterfront. We were also in close proximity to large Japanese barracks in Hongkew. This did not place us in a favorable strategic position.

Everyone in the district fervently hoped, that the pilots were aware that thousands of European refugees lived in the Hongkew district below them. We prayed that they would aim their bombs at the proper Japanese targets around the ghetto, and not drop any on us.

They often came at night, especially when the moon shone brightly, giving them a better view. Frequently we went to bed half dressed, so that we could get ready quickly to go downstairs, when the noise of the air raid sirens combined with anti-aircraft fire from the ground woke us up.

It was all rather frightening and more than a little confusing. Because in spite of the danger we were in, secretly we cheered on the B-29 bombers as they flew high above us. As gradually more and more destruction rained down from the skies, it became clear that the Japanese were taking a beating and the war would hopefully soon come to an end.

There was an infirmary within Ward Road Jail, around the corner from us. Walking along Ward Road, we surreptitiously waved to captured, wounded American flyers, whom we could see behind barred windows. They had been shot down by Japanese anti-aircraft guns during the air raids. Near the end of the war, there was a big commotion when some of the flyers escaped over the high prison walls that were studded with broken glass and barbed wire. The Americans disappeared without a trace. The Japanese searched all over the ghetto for them but did not find them. No doubt, the Americans had a little help from the civilian population.

The worst air raid took place on July 17, 1945, when American B-29 planes aimed for a large Japanese communication station located quite near us. That day some of the bombs also landed directly in the segregated area. Aside from hundreds of Chinese, thirty-one of our people died and several hundred were injured. Many were left homeless and destruction was widespread. The house we lived in on Chusan Road was not hit.

When the air raid was over and the all clear sounded, all available adults and children went out to help the wounded, put out fires, run errands, and do whatever was necessary to bring some order into the existing chaos. That was when the training we had received from local authorities, during air raid drills and bucket brigades, came in handy. We all had some idea of what we had to do.

Most of the houses had no cellars, so during an air raid we always went down to our landlord's rooms on the first floor, where it was thought to be safer. Our so-called air raid shelter consisted of tables pushed together, with mattresses piled on top. Supposedly we were protected from flying debris this way.

While we all crowded together on the floor underneath this arrangement, I sometimes wondered what would happen if we got a direct hit. After all, I thought, no self-respecting bomb would be deterred by a mattress. I never asked that question out loud.

The children coped fairly well with these almost nightly episodes, some of them playing games or even singing, but the adults were usually quite tense during the air raids. Some of the women cried, and others prayed. The pessimists in the group were sure we would all die, while the optimists decided that if we had come this far, we could survive anything.

Often upon hearing the sirens start up their wailing at the beginning of an air raid, my mother just could not deal with it. She was so terrified, that sometimes she was unable to move. Neighbors and my father then carried her downstairs, after calming her down with a few drops of belladonna, prescribed by a sympathetic refugee doctor.

One bright moonlit night, we again left our beds as quickly as we could. We had been awakened by the roar of B-29's followed almost immediately by sirens, sounding a full alert. It was always a toss-up, whether the bombers or the sirens were heard first. The thundering noise of advancing planes together with the high-pitched sound of falling bombs followed by deafening explosions, often preceded the air raid sirens. Sounds like that are not easily forgotten.

Edith and I begged to watch the planes and anti-aircraft fire from our window. We thought it would be a lot more fun to count how many searchlights the bombers would destroy this time, rather than go downstairs and sit under the tables again. But my father would not hear of it and herded us all downstairs.

Later that night, after the all clear siren sounded in the now quiet air, we wearily trooped back into our room. There on my sister's bed, near the window, lay a still smoking white hot piece of shrapnel. A fragment of a bomb which had demolished one of the utility companies near our house, had burned a hole into her pillow, on the exact spot where the indentation of her head still faintly showed. We called it our piece of America and kept it for a good luck piece.

21. GROWING UP IN THE GHETTO

Any time someone had a fight in the house, every word could be heard through the walls and open windows. Tempers were often short, people flared up at the slightest provocation and a lot of arguing went on all the time. Living in cramped, unsanitary surroundings, often with little money or food, life in the ghetto took its toll on people's health and nerves. Our daily life, complicated with worry over relatives left behind in Europe, the struggle to make a living for our family and the uncertainty of our future at the not so tender hands of the Japanese, strained even my father's optimistic nature at times. My mother tried to keep up a pretense of cheerfulness in front of us, but often at night I could hear her crying in bed.

Life was easier for us children. Even though we were well aware of the hardships, we adapted more quickly and just took each day as it came. We had our friends, we went to school, we played games as children do. In general we did not take things too seriously. We were together with our parents, thus we felt protected. Whatever else happened - even if it was unpleasant, was not as terrible for us, as it must have been for them. Throughout, there was always a strong supportive sense of family unity that enveloped us.

It was different with the adults, many of whom had problems adjusting to the extreme climate and the dismal economic conditions. The idea of being fenced in, not knowing what new restrictions and deprivations were still in store for them, made it very hard for some people to cope with their existence. The more enterprising ones drew on all their strength to keep going. Their previous existence had not prepared any of them for the harsh life they found themselves in. Some of the weaker ones, often did not survive life in the ghetto. Tropical diseases, bad health resulting from inadequate diets and living conditions, along with suicides, took their toll.

Sometimes friction came to a boiling point, even between my mother and my aunt. At those times, everybody started yelling and going back to Year One in the family archives, about who did what to whom and when and why. While this was going on, my father in his usual quiet way attempted to make peace. Then my uncle got into the fray and told him to stay out of it. Soon a secondary argument would arise from that. Now all four of them were at it.

Meanwhile, Edith and I tried to stay out of everyone's way. These uprisings were always followed by long crying spells by my mother and my aunt in their respective rooms. A few days later, they had their usual reconciliation ceremony, and everything was fine again for a while.

Nightly blackout regulations were enforced by Japanese patrols, who occasionally entertained themselves by shooting out our lightbulbs, if any stray beams escaped into the street. Like everyone else we had heavy curtains on our two windows, which looked out onto a small alley festooned with laundry drying on bamboo poles.

We also had a perfect view, almost directly into our neighbors' windows. During the long summer twilight before the lights went on, I used to spend a lot of time at my window looking into other people's business.

During that time, when I was about thirteen or fourteen years old, I had the usual curiosity about life and some of the physical changes going on in my body. Many of these questions were answered just by keeping my ears and eyes open to what went on around me. One thing I could not figure out though. Why did the woman in the next house, whose door opened onto the back alley, often greet her gentlemen friends dressed in nothing but her high heels and a necklace?

My girlfriends, whom I sometimes invited to come and look at this awesome sight, offered some wild speculations on the situation.

While my mother carefully explained some things I was brave enough to ask, I got most of my information from my girlfriends. Accurate or not, they seemed to know everything, or at least pretended to. Knowing no better, I believed whatever they told me.

The main thing, we all agreed, was never ever to "do it" no matter how much we liked a boy. I was not too clear on what "doing it" actually was, but I knew it could not be healthy. That fact was clearly brought home to any of us who might be tempted to experiment, when a girl about my age in the neighborhood died of a bungled abortion.

In spite of my parents' attempts at some kind of normalcy, we grew up more quickly than they liked. There was little we did not see or hear. Privacy was a word we did not know the meaning of.

"Illemaus, what are you looking at? You've been at that window for hours," my mother asked.

"Oh nothing, just getting some air," I answered guiltily, as I watched the newlyweds across the alley getting ready for bed. They had forgotten to draw the curtains, giving me a perfect view of the goings-on. It got rather interesting until they spotted me at my lookout post and quickly closed the window.

In the summers when it was too hot to stay indoors, we sat on the front steps of the house, trying to catch a cool breeze before going upstairs to bed. The latest rumors and gossip were exchanged with our neighbors on the street. Under cover of darkness, trading of black market items continued into the night. Many people sold their personal belongings. Jewelry and clothes were bartered away piece by piece, to get extra money. The street was always full of people until curfew time at 10 p.m.

Looking for some extra income, my father and a couple of his friends started a small distillery. They rented a little kitchen around the corner from our house, and hired an old man who knew how to make brandy. Edith and I often went over there to watch the proceedings and sample the goods. Mingled smells of chocolate, coffee and vanilla, not to mention the alcohol, greeted us as soon as we stepped into the room. The old man, who for some reason, always had a very red nose, brewed eggnog, chocolate brandy and coffee brandy. Sometimes we tasted all of it and got a little dizzy. As a special treat, we occasionally took our friends in with us. We became quite popular that year.

The leftover egg-whites from the distillery were taken home in a bucket, and my mother dreamed up new recipes to use them up. They reappeared as very pale scrambled eggs for breakfast. She also whipped them up with a handbeater, for angelfood and sponge cakes. One of us ran downstairs to the *Konditorei* (bakery) to have the cakes baked in their ovens. We had no stove in our little kitchen corner. In any case, our gas and electric were rationed and there was never enough to last until the end of the month.

On Saturdays, when the distillery was closed, my mother

85

sent Edith around the corner, carrying a bulging bag from the market. Just "borrowing" their gas, as she delicately put it. Following Mutti's instructions to finely slice the onions, brown the meat, make sure to add spices and water at the right time, Edith cooked a pot of *goulash* for us. We usually ate that with *nockerl* (tiny dumplings). What a meal!

In the summers, three or four of my girlfriends and I used to walk around the block after supper, before it got too dark. That was accepted as the height of social activity in our age group. If we "accidentally" did not meet the boys going one way, we turned around and went around the block the other way. When we all finally got together, we stood around talking and giggling under one of the few trees in the lane. Sometimes we even shared a forbidden cigarette, passing it around the circle.

We always met the same group of boys during those long twilight hours. I developed a crush on one Russian boy, a couple of years older than myself. I was glad for the fading daylight, because I used to blush if he so much as looked at me. He was more interested in one of my girlfriends though, so I did not blush as often as I would have liked.

This boy lived at the Ward Road Jail around the corner, where his mother worked as a warden. One day he invited our whole group to a tea party at their living quarters inside the jail. We drank tea, ate sandwiches and little cakes, served to us by model prisoners. Afterwards we played Spin-the-Bottle and other kissing games in vogue then. Feeling very daring, I got my first kiss from Igor in the Ward Road Jail.

22. SUNDAY MOVIES

W hile we lived on Chusan Road, my uncle and aunt frequently came from their room next door, to eat a light supper together with us. My family still observed the German custom, of having their main meal, also known as *tiffin* in Shanghai dialect, in the middle of the day and then eat a lighter evening meal.

Tante Liccie and Onkel Erwin used to advance into our room as if they had come from far away, commenting on the weather or inquiring formally into the state of our health. My uncle brought their two sandwiches in a paperbag, my aunt carried her knitting.

My mother made hot tea for us, adding a shot of rum to help us stay warm in the winter. Most of the time, there was an ongoing battle between my father and the potbelly stove in our room. He tried to coax some heat out of the inferior quality coal. The flame usually went out several times and he tried again, striking match after match muttering to himself, all of us shouting encouragement and well meaning advice, as the room filled with smoke. We often went to bed earlier than usual, when there was not enough heat, hurriedly getting under the covers to get warm.

In spite of the hardships in the district, we all tried to carry on a normal lifestyle under the prevailing circumstances. Every day, my father went to his office job, and Edith and I went to school. After Edith got a much longed for bicycle, she often rode it to school. I never had a bike and continued taking the crowded tramcar, with my girlfriends. This often turned out to be quite a treat, on the days when we spotted the handsome, bearded Sikh traffic policeman, who always waved to us on Bubbling Well Road. There he stood in his khaki uniform, a red turban on his head, conducting the traffic like an orchestra. It was worth the long ride to get a smile from him.

The refugees published newspapers and magazines in Hongkew. There were radio shows devoted to programs of interest to the refugees, such as health hints, popular and classical music and local news. Many social and sport events were organized as well as art shows and amateur theatricals. Edith developed quite a knack at ping-pong and made it to the finals. On the high holidays, synagogue services were conducted in rented theaters. Some of the Rabbis and Cantors were familiar to us from Germany.

To improve the neighborhood, the rebuilding of some of the bombed out houses was initiated. Aside from the regular open food market, where my mother bought our vegetables and meat, little shops and coffee houses opened up all over the district. There people could meet and have a cup of coffee and some pastry.

Movies were always well attended and inexpensive. I had always loved the movies and spent many happy hours watching Fred Astaire and Ginger Rogers, Tarzan, Deanna Durbin, Nelson Eddie and Jeanette McDonald to mention just a few. But that was before the Japanese banned American and English movies. During the war years we only saw German, Japanese or Chinese movies.

As a matter of fact, my parents often encouraged Edith and me to go to the movies on weekends, even on rare occasions, when we were not all that eager to go.

"Here's your money, you can even buy a soda. Watch a

double feature if you like. We are just going to take a nap while you are gone."

One Sunday afternoon we returned home earlier than expected, due to the projector breaking down, as it often did. Edith was the first one to walk into the room. She turned right around and came out again. She had apparently caught them in *flagrante delicto*.

"Just trying to keep Mutti warm, nothing to worry about, girls." My father's slightly breathless voice followed us out into the hall. Strange goings on we agreed, as we sat waiting out on the stairs. Sometimes, when my father had a little money left over after payday, he took us all to lunch at one of the refugee restaurants. Once in a while, we also went to the very popular cabaret evenings, where performances by refugee artists always played to sell-out audiences. Closely jammed together, listening to these comedians making jokes about everyday problems or hearing familiar songs sung by professional singers, made people forget where they were and how hard life had really become. Even if only for a little while.

Theater groups were formed that put on whole operettas and plays, performed in rented movie houses in the district. Once when they had a casting call for chorus members, I decided to audition. At home I was always assured that I had a nice voice. In Germany, I was often asked to sing when the family got together, but being rather shy and self-conscious then, I did not often want to do it.

However by now it was already 1944. I was getting older and just beginning to come out of my shell, so I decided to try it. Nervously I made my way through *Red Sails in the Sunset*. As fate would have it, I was completely drowned out by the heavy handed accompanying pianist and nobody heard me.

Someone else with more confidence and possessing no doubt a louder voice than mine, got the part. Such injustice!

23. HAZELWOOD ICE CREAM

One thing that never changed, no matter where we lived, was the daily walk. A habit still so ingrained in my makeup that even now, many years later, if a day passes by without my walk I feel something missing. These constitutionals were usually taken after meals. My mother always said it was healthier for our digestive system. Sometimes, I would have liked to curl up with a good book, but one did not argue with Mutti.

Edith and I with Mutti in the middle, linked arms, adjusted our step, and set out briskly regardless of the weather. If we got out of step we would do a little hop skip and jump and get back in again. One of us was usually bobbing up and down. On our walks, Mutti often entertained us with amusing stories of her youth and the boyfriends she used to have. We always laughed a lot on those outings, because for the time being she would relax and forget her troubles. People we met on the streets often commented on how much we looked like three sisters, instead of mother and daughters. Of course Mutti did not mind that a bit.

One afternoon we planned to visit a friend, who lived near the Japanese barracks. We usually avoided that street, because we tried to stay away from the Japanese as much as we could. Chinese people were required to stop and bow down, when passing the sentries who stood outside the barracks gate. Sometimes, they were kicked if they did not bow low enough.

All three of us looking straight ahead, we quickly passed the sentries standing there with fixed bayonets.

"You, you, come here," came the command in broken English.

"Just keep smiling and don't say anything," my mother whispered nervously as we went over to the guards.

Two soldiers who must have spent a very boring day until we arrived, took their time patting us down from head to toe looking for contraband or whatever, before they let us go. By the time we got home Mutti was hysterical, and we were both crying.

My father complained to the Jewish Community leaders, about what was at the time, a very traumatic episode for us. They reminded him, that there was a war going on, this kind of harrassment was common place and we should watch where we walked next time.

The Japanese had carefully excluded all parks and recreational areas from the designated area. There were few grassy areas or tree-lined avenues to wander around in the district. But by this time, we were used to walking through the streets and did not mind it as much as the older people. They were always longing for a bit of grass and some trees.

Actually it was interesting to walk along and look at the many shops. While there was abject poverty everywhere, the refugees had brought along with them a very strong sense of entrepreneurship and an iron determination to survive and see the end of war and deprivation. Besides the Chinese shops already in existence, many refugees had opened up different stores, some no bigger than a closet. There were many grocery and butcher shops. Some of the stalls in the open air market were operated by enterprising refugees selling food or clothing to Chinese and refugee customers. One could sit at a tiny table in little cafes, where enticing fresh baked goods in the

European tradition were sold with a cup of coffee. Even though the surroundings were shabby the ambiance reminded my parents of Vienna or Berlin. Edith and I were not so concerned with the memories, we were just happy when once in a while we stopped and got a cream puff or some almond pastry.

Right on the sidewalks, an abundance of second-hand clothing was always for sale by refugees, carefully displaying their wares on old newspapers. Beside a Chinese barber shop, you could find a beauty parlor operated by people from Germany. Tailor shops and shoe repair shops owned by refugees or Chinese craftsmen were also plentiful.

One of my prize possessions, when I was about fifteen years old, was a suit, cut down and altered for me from one of my father's suits from Germany. Nothing was ever wasted. When we outgrew our clothes they were cut apart and used as parts of new dresses. My mother did a lot of the sewing herself, dipping into the basket of leftover materials, old buttons, snaps and ribbons that she always saved.

Prodded on by my mother, my father usually came walking with us on Sundays. We looked forward to that, because it meant we might stop at the Chinese ice cream shop. Ice cream was a rare treat for us.

Long blocks of *Hazelwood* ice cream, consisting of chocolate, vanilla and strawberry flavors, were sold in separate slices neatly wrapped in paper. We sat on rough wooden benches and tables, enjoying our refreshing dessert. Like most Chinese shops, the entrance was open to the street. At night, the front of the shop was closed off with wooden shutters. The shopkeeper and his wife, numerous children and sometimes even an ancient grandparent or two, usually lived in the back of the store all crowded together. After the shop closed, they brought out their bedding, to sleep on the tables and benches at night.

Usually we carried our identification papers and our many immunization certificates, when we went outside. Diseases such as typhus, cholera and smallpox were quite common. Little knowledge of disease control filtered down to the Chinese population, especially in the poorer section where we lived. Chinese coolies had a habit of spitting, no one even gave it a second glance. Tossing garbage into the gutter was an accepted practice of Chinese slum life. Often, people could be seen urinating against the side of buildings. Flies were everywhere, rats and roaches quite common place. Combined with the stifling heat in the summer, epidemics took their toll regardless of nationality.

Frequently, medical road blocks supervised by Chinese doctors, appeared on street corners. If you could not produce a current immunization certificate, you were immunized on the spot for whatever disease was out of control at the time. We often made a quick detour, when we had forgotten to carry our immunization papers with us.

Trying to keep up with European standards of cleanliness and hygiene provided quite a challenge to us. Everything we ate had to be washed and kept away from flies. My mother went to the market every day to buy fresh meat and vegetables. We had very little space to keep any fresh food in our room, only a small icebox with a block of ice in it. As the ice melted it dripped into a basin set on the floor below the box. When we were thirsty we always drank tea, usually at room temperature. We never ever drank any water from the tap. Water and milk were always boiled before drinking.

Sometimes my father brought home bottles of soda, but only on special occasions.

Since his childhood, my father had never been in robust health. The extreme climate and the hardships of the ghetto did not make it easier for him. He contracted malaria, and when he had an attack of it he lay in bed shivering with a high fever, while we put compresses on his forehead. With very little medicine available during the war years he just had to get through it, as best as he could.

The worst thing though, was when he occasionally had what he called the colic. Sometimes it was a gallbladder attack and sometimes it was a kidney stone. This usually hit him at night.

With all of us sleeping in the same room he tried not to wake us up. My mother sat with him while he tossed and turned with pain, until finally one of us crept downstairs with a flashlight to the telephone in the hall, and called the doctor. Physicians had special permission enabling them to come out at night during curfew. Like an angel of mercy, the doctor eventually came and gave my father a shot of morphine. Next day we tiptoed around getting ready for school, while my father slept peacefully through the morning.

24. A POSTCARD FROM THERESIENSTADT

E very week, we wrote letters on very thin airmail paper to
our relatives back in Berlin and Czechoslovakia. For a
year or two we received news from them, but after the war
broke out there was only silence. By this time my parents
knew, that no more Jews were allowed out of Nazi occupied
countries. There was no possibility for my grandparents or
any of the uncles and aunts to join us. We all hoped to see
them again after the war was over.

After a long time without any news, it must have been in
1943 or 1944, a postcard came one day to Chusan Road. It
was written by my grandmother Jeanette, who we thought still
lived in Berlin with my grandfather. The card came from a
place called Theresienstadt.

Omi briefly explained that they had been resettled to a
kind of work camp. Without giving any details, she wrote that
she was getting along as best as she could, adding that my
grandfather had died at the camp recently.

I can still hear my mother screaming that day. It reminded
me of the time a few years earlier when we left Berlin, and she
could not bear to leave her parents behind.

Much later, when Mutti could talk about it, she told us
that my grandfather had served with the German Army in
World War I. He had been stationed in a barracks in
Theresienstadt and spent much of his time in the army there.

Resourceful as ever, the Germans turned it into a con-
centration camp during the second World War.
Theresienstadt was used for propaganda purposes by the
Nazis. They conducted tours for news media from different

96

countries, showing what a model resettlement camp they had built, for benefit of the Jews. In reality it was a work camp, using forced labor extracted from Jewish prisoners. It also served as a staging area for removal to death camps of the inmates who survived the brutal conditions there. My mother's parents and thousands of others died there.

We were not aware of these events during the war years. Rumors about concentration camps and wholesale slaughter that sometimes drifted along, were not believed, simply because they were so unbelievable. It was only later, when it was all over, that the incredible facts emerged.

After the war ended, my father made many inquiries through the Red Cross trying to trace the whereabouts of our relatives. Eventually, we found out that almost the whole family was wiped out. Some of them could not be traced at all and were never heard from again. Both sets of grandparents, one in Theresienstadt and the other somewhere in a Polish concentration camp, along with the uncles, the aunts and their children had been exterminated. With few exceptions, the cousins I had played with years ago in Czechoslovakia were gone. They died alone, or together with their parents, we never knew. All we could find out was that they were transported to concentration camps in Poland.

Only three of my father's family survived the camps. They were his brother Artur, sister Irma, and my cousin Otto. All my mother had left of hers was her sister Liccie, with us in Shanghai, and her brother Ernst who had fled to England before the war. Tante Grete, her oldest sister who had refused to leave my grandparents alone in Berlin, was also killed with her husband in one of the camps, probably in Poland.

25. THE WOES OF WINTER

Substandard living conditions in the segregated district, where people were often cold and hungry, along with the terror of the increasing bombing raids, took their toll on the health of the ghetto residents. The years of 1944 and early 1945, were the worst, as far as the mortality rate in the district was concerned. Many of the older people did not survive that winter. Disease and malnutrition were widespread. Even though our local hospital in the Ward Road *Heim* had a hard-working staff, there was not enough medicine or equipment to take care of our needs. It was a very difficult task to supply medical care for so many people at once, complicated by the fact that many of them suffered from tropical diseases largely unknown to doctors trained in Europe.

Intense cold combined with an infection wiped out half a dozen infants in the maternity ward one winter night. The newborn baby of my dentists, a husband and wife team, was among them. After many problems and miscarriages, they had finally become parents only to lose that child also.

After school, I used to walk to the tiny dental office they had opened in their Hongkew home. There they attempted to straighten out my teeth which were growing in a rather haphazard fashion. Judging by the results they eventually obtained, I don't know how well trained they were for this procedure, but these two very nice people were all that were available to me at that time.

My teeth were covered with silver caps, that had little hooks attached to them. My job was to anchor little rubber bands to these contraptions. The bands usually popped off and landed in my food. While I had this cumbersome apparatus in my mouth, I took care never to talk or smile in public. I thought I was really ugly, and certainly did not wish to draw attention to myself. My self-confidence, not one of my strong points anyway, definitely needed a boost.

During that terrible last winter of the war, my mother became ill with an intestinal disease, complicated by pneumonia. Admitting her to the local hospital, with it's poor conditions, was not even considered an option. Fortunately doctors in those days still made housecalls, so after much discussion between my parents and our doctor, I was appointed to be my mother's nurse.

Over the objections of my school's headmaster, who seemed to feel that I had untapped potential, I was taken out of the Shanghai Jewish School and put in charge of the household. I was just fifteen years old.

Even though I was a fairly good student, particularly in subjects I liked, I don't remember ever being very happy in school. As a matter of fact I was always plotting ways to get out of school. I had some friends among the Russian girls in my class, but the uncomfortable feeling that I did not really belong, was always there in the back of my mind. It was also decided, that my sister who was in her final year at school and doing well, would stay on to complete her studies.

I can remember sitting next to my mother's bed that winter, in our room on Chusan Road. Trying to feed her, talking to her, washing and changing her when she was too weak to do it herself, beside keeping house for my father and my sister occupied my time. There were always books to read from the library. During those long hours I sometimes read two or three books in one day. I was glad to be out of school, quite content to be where I was needed most. In later years, we could even joke that in spite of my nursing care, Mutti eventually recovered from her illness, while the long winter was coming to an end.

26. A PLATONIC AFFAIR

It was August 1945. Finally at long last, the war was really over. What everyone had hoped and prayed for had come to pass. We were free. Free to come and go as we pleased, free to live wherever we chose to again.

It was as if the earth had suddenly swallowed up the Japanese soldiers, who had been so much in evidence until then. Gone were the patrols checking our passes around the designated area. Gone the barbed wire barricades at the exit gates. The Chinese Nationalist Government was back in power, and the Japanese Army quickly disappeared from the streets. They were not looking for any confrontations with the Chinese inhabitants they had humiliated for so long. When the former military commander of the ghetto, Mr. Ghoya, imprudently ventured out of doors, he got a terrible beating from some of the refugee youths. They had their own score to settle with him.

Liberation also came at last, to the many American, British and other enemy nationals, who had been imprisoned by the Japanese forces in detention camps on the outskirts of Shanghai. Everyone celebrated. The streets in Hongkew were filled with singing and dancing. Total strangers hugged each other in their happiness and relief. Prayer meetings were held to give thanks that we were still alive and to remember those who had perished.

Impatient as we were to leave our rented room on Chusan Road, still a few months went by until my father and mother could organize and finance such a move. At last moving day came. We hired some Chinese coolies who carried our belongings on their pushcarts over to our very own house, located in Joseph's Court, on Kwenming Road. We followed in rickshaws also piled high with suitcases.

Our new home was one of a group of row houses built around a large courtyard, with a plot of grass and flowers in the middle of it. A Sikh security man wearing the usual bright red turban, acted as watchman at the entrance gate. Even though it was a small house with only four or five rooms, it was quite a change from what we had been used to.

We finally had a kitchen downstairs, and our very own bathroom on the second floor, next to the room Edith and I shared. My parents slept in an alcove in the large living room downstairs, on the old couches brought over from Chusan Road. There was even a built-in tenant who lived on the top floor in a little room with a big padlock on his door. He came with the house when my parents bought it. He was a polite fellow and his rent came in handy with the family finances. We were all quite happy with our new living arrangements.

My mother by now, had recovered from her illness. She had not set foot outside the district for years. Finally she was free to go out anywhere she liked. Together we often took a tramcar into the city of Shanghai. We walked in the parks, we looked at all the large department stores, sometimes we went to the movies.

One hot summer day, the American fleet came steaming into the harbor, with flags flying and bands playing. I was in town with some of my girlfriends, walking along Nanking Road. Like a mighty tide, American sailors, soldiers and marines on their first shore leave, came pouring off the ships. They rode into town in rickshaws, pedicabs and taxis. Judging by the noise they made, celebrating was definitely on their minds. People on the street stopped and stared, shopkeepers hung out hastily acquired American flags, little Chinese children scrambled around for chewing gum and candy, thrown to them by the victorious Americans. The whole place was in an uproar.

The Americans whistled and called to us in very free and friendly fashion. Obviously they had not seen any girls for a long time. Half falling out of their rickshaws they were yelling: "Give us a smile, Red." I had no idea what they meant, it did not occur to me that they referred to my red hair. They complimented us on our looks and asked us for dates. We were enthralled and flattered.

So this was what the Americans were like! Quite a difference from the serious, parent-approved boys we knew at home. When we saw what was going on out there, we told ourselves to get ready for it. A whole new world was opening up.

My sister and I had sometimes gone to a dance or a picnic with the local boys at home. They became more attentive as I got older and a little more sure of myself. Once a group of us went up to the Roy Roof-Garden Cafe to dance. Encouraged by flattery of some of the young men at our table, I entered an ongoing "Miss Hongkew" beauty contest. Teetering unsteadily on my high heels, wearing a blue homemade cotton dress, I paraded around the little dance floor with the other girls, under twinkling lights strung up on bamboo poles. I think I got second or third prize that night.

Edith, by that time, had a boyfriend who sold fountain pens in a little shop. He used to come over on his bicycle to visit her. Manfred planned to marry my sister after he had saved a thousand dollars. Unfortunately the poor chap, a serious young man with a mother and two sisters to support, could not sell his fountain pens fast enough. Edith went off to work for the Americans and that was the last she saw of Manfred.

The American Armed Forces made their headquarters in Shanghai, taking over many of the larger buildings and hotels in the city. We wasted no time applying for the many jobs suddenly available. Most of our girlfriends also started to work for the Americans and made friends with them, often leaving behind local boyfriends for the dazzle and glamor of the military.

That was the time I started to use a different first name. My legal name was Ilse Margot Kohn, but I had one more name. One I had never used until then, and that was Betty. By now of course, we had already dropped Sara, the middle name the Germans had made us use. Anyway, I put all my names down on my job application. The Americans picked out the ones easiest for them to pronounce and suddenly I was Betty I. Kohn.

Who's that? I had never seen this combination before, but I liked the sound of it and have used variations of it ever since. At home though, my family took little notice of all these changes. I was still called Ille or Illemaus, just as usual.

Moreover, I added on a few years to my rather tender age. Even I could see, that at barely sixteen years of age I might be too young to be hired. Soon I had a job selling goods at the Signal Corps P.X. stationed at the old German School (Kaiser Wilhelm Schule) in the Western District.

The first thing I did when I got there was to tear up pictures of Hitler, which were still lying around. To say that I enjoyed working there is probably an understatement. Not only did I get paid in real American dollars, vastly superior to the constantly devaluating Chinese currency, but I met the nicest people.

The men outnumbered the girls by about ten to one. Most of my girlfriends and I had more offers for dinner dates and dances than we could handle. We learned to do the jitterbug and the conga, we dressed up in our handmade silk dresses sewn by Chinese tailors, we put gardenias in our hair, painted our nails and bought *Tangee* lipsticks. With the money I earned, I bought my first gray lamb-skin fur coat. I wore snakeskin leather high heeled pumps, made to order for me by a Chinese shoemaker. They matched the coat perfectly.

It was all very satisfying and I had the time of my life. Depending on whom we went out with, we would go to the Enlisted Men's Club or to the Officer's Club after we got off from work. Sometimes our dates picked us up at home, driving in their Army jeeps. When they brought us home again, our Indian watchman always seemed to come by on his rounds just as we bid our dates goodnight on our front porch. It was a very exciting time to be young.

These young servicemen came from completely different backgrounds than we did, and places we knew little about. It was fascinating to hear about their lives and the homes they came from in America, just as they were interested in the way we lived.

Edith was by now working in the Broadway Mansion, as a dispatcher for the American Air Force. Coming home at night after a date, we used to giggle and compare notes on our current boyfriends, until my parents would tell us to be quiet so they could get some sleep.

One night her date missed the last military bus back to his

base. Edith graciously invited him to stay overnight. She sneaked him past my sleeping parents, only to lock the poor guy up in the meter room. Every house had a small concrete-floored room that contained the electric and gas meter. He had to sleep on one of our old steamer trunks from Germany, huddled in a blanket because it was so cold in there. In the morning she fortunately remembered to let him out again. Turning down her offer of breakfast, he left in a hurry never to be heard from again.

Among all the people I met at that time, one in particular stands out head and shoulders above the rest. As even my mother said so poetically in German, after she met him: "*Da kann man Vater und Mutter vergessen.*" More or less this means that the sight of him makes you forget who your parents are.

She was absolutely right. I was quite definitely in love with Patrick. It was as if the sun rose and set with him. One day he walked into the P.X. where I worked. *Holiday for Strings* played on the U.S. Army radio station. I looked up and there he was, looking right at me. I will never forget that moment. He wanted to buy some shampoo, but I had just lost my heart and did not even hear what he said.

Pat was a lieutenant in the Signal Corps. A handsome young man with wavy brown hair and a smile that crinkled up around his bright blue eyes, he wore his uniform as if born to it. It was not long before we dated each other exclusively. As he was in his early twenties, I let him think that I was already eighteen years old myself. I had no intention of letting my tender years become a problem here. Pat came from a small Southern town in the United States, he spoke with a strong Southern accent. Like everything else about him, this completely captivated me. It did not even matter, that I did not always understand what he was saying.

We went for long walks, took pedicab rides sitting close together, holding hands. In the evenings we used to go out to dinner and dancing at the Officer's Club, or to some of the fashionable nightclubs in Shanghai. We chose our very own song, namely: *You Came Along From Out Of Nowhere*. Whenever the band played it, we would dance together cheek to cheek, singing the words to each other. It was just like in the movies. I wished it would never end.

One romantic evening we strolled around in the moonlit garden of the French Club during the orchestra's intermission. It was a Valentine's Day Dance, all perfect with hearts and flowers. I had never even heard of this holiday before, it was all new and exciting to me. I thought, this surely must be heaven.

It was then he suggested that we embark on a platonic relationship. A platonic what? I had absolutely no idea what he meant, but if that was what he wanted, well then it was good enough for me. I looked it up in a dictionary later on, but I was still somewhat mystified.

Shortly after that night, his unit was sent back home to the States and I was left alone. I missed him terribly. I was very unhappy, locked myself in my room and cried for days. Secretly I had hoped to marry him, but he apparently was not ready for that. His plans were to finish college and help his parents after he got home. Plans that did not include me.

Ultimately I returned to the Laidlaw Business School, where I was by now enrolled to learn "a proper profession" as my father put it. Showing up there after the big farewell, still sniffling and red-eyed, the nice little English lady who taught typing and shorthand, sympathetically assumed that I must

have had a death in the family. She excused me for the day. I
went home and cried some more.

27. NOW IS THE HOUR

During the time the Occupying Forces were in Shanghai, many lasting friendships were formed with local inhabitants. These friendships frequently led to a number of weddings between American servicemen and girls living in Shanghai. It was not a simple procedure to get married, because the American authorities would research, very thoroughly, the girl's background and previous political affiliations, if any, before allowing such a marriage to take place. At the same time, often the girl's family tried to make inquiries into the background of their daughter's fiancee. Seeing that these young men came from half-way around the world, obtaining reliable information was sometimes quite difficult.

I attended several weddings of my girlfriends to American servicemen in Shanghai. At one of these affairs, where I was the maid of honor, the girl's parents who were Orthodox Jews, had refused permission for the marriage because the bridegroom was of another religion. They disowned their daughter and boycotted the ceremony. Nonetheless, the tearful but determined bride appeared in a borrowed dress, wearing a bit of window curtain for a veil, and the wedding proceeded without her parents. Soon after that the young couple went to America together.

With few exceptions, most of the people we knew wanted emigrate to America. Those people who had sponsors in America and who had favorable quota numbers, left as soon as they could after the war ended. From 1948 on, many others went to the newly proclaimed State of Israel, which had

109

established an open door policy for anyone of Jewish background who wanted to emigrate there. Some of the Russians decided to return to the U.S.S.R. Other people chose to go back to Europe. But for the most part the place of choice was America.

After Patrick left and the few letters he wrote to me gradually dwindled away into a crashing silence, it finally dawned on me that our romance was really over. He was not going to send for me as I had fondly hoped. I made a determined effort, pulled myself together and went on with my life.

Not lacking for male companionship in those days, two or three times I cheerfully said <u>yes</u>, when a romantic G.I. or Marine contemplated marriage. I liked the idea of being engaged to some nice attentive person, but I must not have been very serious about actually getting married. All the attention was probably good for my still somewhat bruised ego.

When inevitably my future mate and I would come to a parting of the ways, I sometimes had a fleeting suspicion, quickly pushed aside of course, that perhaps they too, were just a bit relieved at the way things worked out in the end.

I think most of the fellows were just as inexperienced as I was. We all swam around in a sea of romance, seeing ourselves in a little house with a picket fence in some enchanting little town, without the slightest clue of how that would all come about. We were all so young, so dazzled by the times, the place and the taste of our newfound freedom. Trying to put the harsh war years behind us, we threw ourselves into romantic, sometimes wishful thoughts where moon always rhymed with June, there was a handsome prince waiting around the bend just for us, and all marriages were made in heaven. You walked up the aisle and life would be all sunshine and bliss forever, just like in the movies.

Sometimes when I complained to my mother that I would definitely be an old maid and never find the right person to marry, she used to say: "Don't worry Illemaus, you are your mother's daughter and just like I did, you will find the one just for you. Now do you want to come into the kitchen and learn to cook and bake?"

By then I was eighteen years old, without having to lie about my age anymore, working as a secretary in Shanghai business offices. The atmosphere at work was stimulating and interesting for me, also I went out most evenings and was having fun. I must have given my parents some sleepless nights while I danced and dined my way around town. I was definitely not interested in the complexities of taking apart a chicken, or what was the best way to make a *strudel*.

About that time, my sister started paying attention to the saying that the way to a man's heart is through his stomach. She began listening closely to my mother, intent on learning the art of housekeeping. Edith was engaged to a young G.I. stationed with the American Military Police in Shanghai. Jim often came to our house and not only because he liked the food. Far away from his home he enjoyed the family atmosphere. We all often sat around on our little roof garden singing along with him, as he played country music on his guitar.

Edith and Jim got married in the spring of 1948, in the Enlisted Men's Club at the Shanghai Race Course. In a short civil ceremony my sister became an American dependent. About half a year later, with the Chinese Communists close to taking over Shanghai, she and Jim were repatriated to the United States.

My parents and I went to see them off at the docks on the Bund. An American army band played *Now is the Hour*, as the large troop transport slowly pulled out into the Whangpoo River. Every time I hear that song, it brings back that farewell on a raw November day.

It was to be five years before my sister and I saw each other again. Earlier that year my Aunt Liccie and Uncle Erwin had gotten the necessary papers together and left for America, where they eventually settled down in Boston, Massachussetts. Only my parents and I were left in Shanghai, of the group that left Germany nine years earlier.

28. A MATTER OF CHOICE

"What do you mean you're going to marry this man? You said this a few times before already and then changed your mind, so that means you don't know what you want, and besides you've only known him for two weeks. We never even heard of him, and what an unpronounceable name he has! Can you imagine what your children will have to go through? Anyway, he is a White Russian and they don't marry Jews, especially not German refugees."

On and on it went. Although I was not about to admit it to my parents, I really knew very little about the object of their concern. What I did know however, I definitely liked.

The usual August heat and humidity was at it's peak that Shanghai summer of 1948. As I came out into the street after leaving my air conditioned office in the Glenline Building, where I worked as a secretary with the U.S. Navy Supply Department, I was immediately enveloped by hot sticky air.

I loved my job and got along well with the other people in the office. I had plenty of friends and quite an active social life. Consequently, I was quite contented with things at that point, and not on the lookout for any forays into the unknown. Little did I know how my life was about to change. On the spur of the moment, I decided to go for a swim before going home for the day. Catching a rickshaw, I was soon on my way to the Race Course swimming pool.

As I swam around in the cool, refreshing water in my German style breast stroke, I was offered some points on how better to stay afloat by the handsome, muscular lifeguard on duty. In his Russian accent, Oleg Dimitrievich Grebenschikoff introduced himself.

"I'll never remember how to pronounce a name like that." I laughed. He handed me his name card, then asked me for a date that night.

"I won't be home for dinner tonight." I informed my mother. "There's a crazy Russian here who wants me to go to dinner with him. He's tall and good looking, quite different from anyone I've ever met."

On the telephone my mother warned me darkly to keep my wits together and stay out of trouble. She would wait up for me, she added.

Oleg was a Physical Education teacher at the Shanghai Jewish School, the same school that I left just before he started teaching there. My sister actually met him before I did. She once attended a function at the Russian Club, where she and Oleg got into conversation. He asked her for a date, she accepted, but for some reason she did not follow through with the arrangement. The next time she saw him, she was already married to Jim, and Oleg and I were getting engaged.

A champion swimmer and superb athlete, sports of any kind were Oleg's main interest in life. Soon after we were married, he left school teaching to become Physical Director at the Y.M.C.A. in Shanghai. He always referred to himself as a Y.M.C.A. man.

The Y.M.C.A. was a mixture of a social and athletic club. Housed in a large building on Nanking Road facing the Shanghai Race Course, it contained a bowling alley, a swimming pool next to the gymnasium, a large ballroom and many areas for sitting and chatting with friends. Traditional English afternoon tea poured from a silver service, was served by Chinese waiters daily in the well-stocked library. There were several floors for residents upstairs, as well as a variety of select shops and restaurants on the ground floor.

Often we would *rendez-vous* in the American style coffee-shop downstairs, to drink coffee and eat chocolate log cake with our friends. This Y.M.C.A. setting provided a base, serving as a meeting place for Oleg and his contemporaries, ever since he was a young boy. When I met him he lived in rented rooms in Shanghai, but the "Y" was in every way his home away from home.

His widowed mother put Oleg and his brother Igor into a British boarding school, soon after her arrival in Shanghai from Manchuria, in 1926. The two boys were too young to go to school, but she did not want to leave them alone with Chinese servants while she worked. As both were big for their age, she stretched the truth a bit and got them admitted without showing their birth certificates. She pretended that all her papers were lost during her travels. The result was, that for years they were not sure how old they really were.

Oleg loved his years in the Public and Thomas Hanbury School and later at St. John's University. School life suited him well. He even kept fond memories of lining up for a spoonful of cod-liver oil every day, not to mention the pillow fights and some of the other mischief, like soap skating across the shower room floors, for which he sometimes got a caning on his bottom from the supervisors.

His Siberian forebears' high cheekbones and solid bone structure, earned him the nickname of Big Head or Lug, in school. His younger brother Igor, built along the same lines but in a slightly smaller edition, was known as Small Head.

From the time Oleg was a boy he knew he wanted to be a teacher. A handsome, personable young man who carried himself well, Oleg had a quick sense of humor that came across in any of the languages he spoke: Russian, English and Chinese, and also in the half dozen others he pretended to speak. He had many friends of different nationalities and backgrounds, and a knack of being completely at home in any situation. When I met him he was one of the most popular and eligible bachelors in town, a fact of which I duly took note.

With our courtship progressing rapidly, my father made discreet inquiries among his friends and business associates, about this fellow who monopolized his daughter's time and total attention. Grudgingly, he finally admitted that he could not find anything wrong with him, except for the difficulties we would doubtless encounter arising from differences in our background, religion and nationality.

Oleg's mother, meanwhile also took some time getting used to the idea that her oldest son cast aside tradition and motherly advice, and had chosen a bride different in every way to what she had in mind for him.

I have a vivid memory of our first meeting. Hoping to make a good impression, I dressed carefully and had my hair done at the Nanking Road Barber Shop. Then Oleg took me to lunch at Mrs. Speelman's apartment, a lady friend of his who made her living cooking Russian meals for paying guests. Thus fortified, we finally went to see his mother. All of us standing around awkwardly, he introduced me to her as her future daughter-in-law.

The poor lady turned pale, she was completely taken aback. This was the last thing she expected. Thinking about it later I could see that we might have broken the news to her a little more diplomatically. But when you are in love, you expect the whole world to feel the same way you do about the object of your affection.

"So this is the reason why you have not even phoned me in the last two weeks? You were too busy to give your mother any time."

Thoroughly intimidated I stood there, clutching the bouquet of flowers I forgot to hand to her, while I fervently wished myself to be somewhere else. Fortunately, she eventually rallied and decided to make the best of it; once she realized that we were quite serious about the marriage.

She, and my equally apprehensive parents, met at a dinner party at *Sun Ya's* restaurant. All of us were on our absolutely best behavior, with smiles and pleasantries all around. Then she proceeded to supervise the making of my wedding dress at her shop, called Madame Greenhouse.

My developing relationship with her was one of restrained respect mixed with a cool tolerance on her part. It took us both some years before we managed to put these feelings aside, but ultimately, we felt comfortable enough with each other to become friends.

29. MADAME GREENHOUSE

If you wanted stylish clothes with a certain flair, the kind that made other women mutter: "I'll bet she got that at Madame Greenhouse," you would save your money and willingly hand it over to the woman who was to be my mother-in-law, Alexandra Vassilievna Grebenschikoff, known as Kisa to her friends, of Madame Greenhouse.

Just walking into the shop and meeting Kisa was quite an experience. She was born in Russia to an upper middle-class family, educated in the best schools where she learned English, French and German, which she liberally sprinkled into her Russian accented speech. You needed an alert ear to follow her conversation as it rolled along. "My dear, you absolutely must try this new *crepe de Chine*, it is just so *chic, nicht wahr*?" she would exclaim in her melodious voice.

Kisa herself was always perfectly turned out. When I first met her she was probably in her late forties, usually wearing linen suits with silk shirts, her hair upswept into a chignon, make-up always perfectly applied. Kisa carried herself very straight which made her look taller than she actually was. She had beautiful hands and feet, her nails always flawlessly manicured. She always wore a black onyx ring, said to be an heirloom. Kisa was a handsome woman, not beautiful in the classic sense, but possessing an elegance and style all of her own.

She ran that dress shop like a well oiled machine. From the several tailors in the back room, she would majestically summon what she referred to as her Number One Tailor.

"Number One, you come please," she would call out to

him, and Number One proud of his exalted position, came running from his supervisory duties in the sewing room. Neatly dressed in his long blue Chinese gown, armed with pincushion and measuring tape, he presented himself in the showroom. Together they performed their miracles with silks and satins, to the delight of the customers.

While Kisa, helped by the smiling Number One, fitted me for my wedding dress, she talked about her life. "I married very young in life," she said, lifting the heavy French satin over my head. "Where are the pearls you will sew on the veil, Number One?"

"I promise Madame, I order. Come tomollow, velly velly sure, no ploblem." The smiling tailor replies in his Pidgin English.

"Ah *spasiba* (thank you), now where was I? Oh yes," she goes on without missing a beat. "My husband was an officer in the Czar's army when we lived in Vladivostok. Ah, the parties and the life there, so very - how you say? - so very graceful, such elegance. But of course it all came to an end. The Communist revolution finally caught up with us out there in Siberia," Kisa recalled, with a faraway look in her eyes, "and in 1922 we ran away to Manchuria with my little son. Oh, *mon dieu* - how I cried for my mother and my sisters Genia and Vera, who stayed behind in Russia."

Turning me around deftly to make sure my dress hung properly, she continues ordering Number One Tailor around: "Here put in a tuck and there, Missy very slim, I want her to look like the Czarina herself, very regal and majestic."

Number One complies. He seems not too sure what a Czarina is, but he is agreeable to anything Kisa says. She finally continued her story at my urging.

"My husband died a few years later in that terrible place in the city of Mukden, in Manchuria." She stops for a moment, a tear rolls down her cheek. Number One whips out a beautifully clean linen handkerchief and hands it to her.

She smiles at him and continues: "What a dusty and provincial place, no proper medical care, no culture there at all. I was left alone, almost penniless, with my two little boys Oleg and Igor. They are named after two Russian princes, you know," she says proudly. "Ignorant about money as I was in those days, after my husband died I was swindled out of his furniture business by his partner. So in 1926, I took my sons, got on a train and traveled down to Shanghai, where I had old friends that I knew from Russia."

Kisa smiled, "You see Number One Tailor here?" Number One draws himself up to his full height, fully conscious of his place in the scheme of things. He has heard this story many times but he never gets tired of it. His fierce loyalty to Kisa shone in his eyes.

"Just like him, I learned every aspect of the dressmaking business. As a widow, I had to work very hard to provide for my sons and myself." Kisa continued. "They grew up in boarding school, and I lived in a rented room in my friend's house. I used to visit my boys on Sundays and bring them Russian candy I made myself. They always cried when I left them, and I did too."

The years went by. Her sons grew up, and Kisa through hard work and determination eventually became the manager of Madame Greenhouse, Number One always at her beck and call.

Old *Shanghai Hands* remember her well. Some of the lucky ones still have a dress or a coat that she made for them at

Madame Greenhouse at 790, Bubbling Well Road. My wedding gown made from the finest French satin, wrapped up like a mummy in folds of tissue paper, is packed away in the old Chinese camphor chest.

"This gown will last a lifetime or longer, and your daughters will wear it too," I can almost hear Kisa say. And as always, she was quite right.

30. MARRIED LIFE

Less than three months after we met, Oleg and I were married. Twice! One week prior to our so-called real wedding, a civil ceremony at a Chinese lawyer's office was performed to satisfy the many legal requirements of the Chinese authorities. Following the short ceremony we celebrated with some friends at a Chinese restaurant. We showed off our fancy legal wedding scrolls, generously illustrated with many beaming Chinese cherubs happily beating on drums, while others danced around carrying red flags and lanterns. The whole document was edged with flowers and birds. Our names were in English, but the text of the document was in Chinese. Somewhat reluctantly, we then followed my parents' instructions and repeated advice; both returning to our respective homes to meet again a week later for the second wedding.

After being turned down by the Russian Orthodox Church and the Jewish religious authorities, we discovered that the Union Church, located near the Soochow Creek, would perform the marriage ceremony without requiring either one of us changing to the other's religion.

Oleg and I agreed before the marriage, that we would each keep our faith and raise our future children open to both our religions and backgrounds.

After a wedding reception at the Y.M.C.A. ballroom, we left for our honeymoon in Hangchow, several hours train ride away from Shanghai. Favored by many as a honeymoon hideaway, it was a beautiful spot by the peaceful West Lake, surrounded by mountains and lush valleys. With it's many temples, pagodas, pavilions and tea rooms under the weeping willow trees by the lake, it was a place much beloved by poets and scholars throughout the ages. This was the first of countless journeys we took together in the decades that followed.

We launched into married life amidst a sea of political upheaval in China. There was mounting concern about the future of course, but having gotten through the war we felt that we could overcome whatever happened. Nothing could be as bad, we were sure, as what we had already experienced.

The Chinese Communists had been fighting the Nationalists for years in the interior. By 1949, the Communist Army was advancing slowly but surely toward Shanghai. It was inevitable that within a short time they would enter the city. Along with other foreigners in Shanghai, we became uncomfortably aware that our days in China were numbered.

Where to go? What to do? It was time to make a move to another country again. This was not easy. Our choices were very limited. Not having the necessary quota numbers excluded us from going to the U.S.A. Going back to Soviet Russia was out of the question for my husband. As the son of a Russian officer who had served under the Czar, his safety there appeared questionable. Some of the Shanghai Russians went back and were never heard from again. Israel was open to us by that time thanks to the law of return for Jews and their spouses, but living conditions were very harsh there. Before making a decision, we waited to see what other opportunities would present themselves.

My parents who still lived in Hongkew, hoped to go to America as soon as their paperwork was completed at the American Consulate. In the meantime my sister, by now settled in America with her husband, had found a sponsor who was willing to act as their guarantor.

In spite of all the uncertainties surrounding us, life went on with some degree of normalcy. Oleg and I now lived in the Y.M.C.A. residential quarters in a room overlooking the Race Course. He was in charge of the Y.M.C.A. Sports Department and I was still working with the U.S. Navy at the Glenline Building on the Bund.

Initial attempts at impressing my new husband with my less than perfect cooking skills, were often punctuated by frantic telephone calls to my mother for advice. Not conducive to my efforts was the little kerosene stove balanced on the window-sill, on which I tried to bring forth something edible. While the cooker had to be pumped furiously to get it going, the pungent kerosene fumes mingled with my culinary efforts. Once I nearly caused a major disaster when the curtains caught fire during one of these experiments. We almost always ate in the Y dining room after that.

On Sundays we usually went to the Race Course and watched the soccer or softball games, in which Oleg also often played. Sometimes we played some tennis, then we all gathered to eat a *tiffin* of chicken curry at the Race Course restaurant, liberally washed down by jugs of *shandy* (beer and lemonade mixed).

There was a very strong friendship and team spirit among the group that usually gathered together those afternoons. Mostly they had all grown up together and gone to the same schools. Often we all finished off the evening having dinner together at the Y, then going to a movie or a party at someone's house.

Coming from Hongkew, which was considered by some to be on the other side of the tracks, I was something of a newcomer in the crowd. German Jews from Hongkew and what was known as the Foreign Y crowd, which included members of old established Shanghai families, did not generally mix too much as a rule. They each had their own particular social clubs and entertainment and usually tended to stay within their own circle.

Finding myself in this new society, my initial reserve was soon replaced by a confidence, that came with being married to one of the leaders of the group. I soon got into the spirit of my new life. I started to enjoy my status as a newlywed with an attentive husband and many new friends. They welcomed me and helped make my transition easier. Some of the friendships formed at that time, lasted for years over distance and time.

It took me a little while though, to get used to being surrounded by crowds of people all the time. They always kept up an easy conversation, all laughing uproariously at the same jokes, repeating them time after time. They went everywhere together as a group, usually making their presence known with a lot of high-spirited noise and good-natured bantering.

31. THE LIBERATION OF SHANGHAI

Carefully keeping out of sight, we pulled aside heavy velvet curtains draping the tall windows of the Foreign Y.M.C.A. facing Nanking Road. What the Chinese Communist Army chose to call the Battle of Liberation, was in full swing below us on the street. Shooting had been going on all night. By afternoon there was little resistance left, only sporadic gunshots pierced the air.

As we watched in disbelief, a number of Nationalist Army soldiers crouching in the sandbagged pillbox in front of the building, shed their uniforms and laid down their rifles. Dressed in the long pyjama-type pants commonly worn by Chinese, they disappeared swiftly into winding back alleys in the fading daylight, to avoid being taken prisoner by the advancing Communist army.

Just a few days ago, we were sitting in the Grand Theater near the Y.M.C.A. watching Laurence Olivier in the movie *Hamlet*. Suddenly the performance was interrupted by cannon fire. For a moment we were not sure whether the noise came from the screen or from outside, but soon we found out that this was not make-believe. I watched *Hamlet* many times again, but I will always remember the first thunderous version I saw in Shanghai, as being just a little different from the others.

For many anxious hours we had no word from my parents in Hongkew. Finally we established telephone contact. They assured us they were safe and that their part of town had also been "liberated" by the Communists.

After taking the city, the Communist Army arranged a

victory parade along the Bund. Brand-new Chinese flags waved in the breeze. Schools and businesses closed for the day, and thousands of people came out and cheered. Pictures and slogans of Mao-Tse-Tung were everywhere.

All sorts of new rules and regulations were proclaimed for all the inhabitants to follow. A crackdown on collaborators and enemies of the new government, resulted in public hangings on hastily built scaffolds right out on busy street corners. For a while we did not dare go out, there was so much confusion and disorder all around.

The good life for foreigners in China had definitely ended. What had once been a sanctuary, an established way of life for old *China Hands* who had lived in the country for generations, and also for the later influx of European refugees, gradually turned into a threatening existence for us all. Anti-foreign sentiment was on the rise. Our safety became doubtful. Everyone redoubled their efforts to leave the country as soon as possible. Bureaucratic red tape required by the Communists, when one wanted to leave was overwhelming, added on to that was all the paperwork required by the countries people applied to for emigration. Time was of the essence, particularly for Oleg and myself. After suffering a miscarriage in the first year of our marriage, I was now well into my second pregnancy and again experiencing some problems. I had orders to rest and think pleasant thoughts. Instead of that I worried and ate too much, justifying to myself that I had to eat for two now. More than anything we wanted our baby to be born in a friendly and peaceful country, removed from all the strife and upheavals that had marked both our childhoods.

We recalled that Oleg's mother had an old friend in

Australia whom she corresponded with. After some coaxing, this lady, a Mrs. Sudakoff, agreed to be our sponsor if we wanted to immigrate there. As we had very few realistic choices and a very limited time in which to act, we accepted her offer very quickly. At the same time I was only too well aware, that I would be going far away from my own family, some already in America, others making plans to go there.

After filling out mountains of applications, culminated by a long interview with the Australian consul who was just about to close his country's consulate in Shanghai, Oleg and I finally had our papers. We got ready to leave for Sydney. Oleg's mother and brother planned to follow us a few weeks later.

Under the auspices of the International Refugee Organization, we became part of a group leaving Shanghai by train. The head of this organization was on old schoolmate of Oleg's, one Lorenzo Lo. He asked Oleg to take charge of our group consisting of about thirty people. Oleg's job was to watch out for them, help them with their documents, their luggage, their questions, until we would arrive in Hongkong.

Because of rumors that the Shanghai harbor was mined, no ships could enter or leave port. So the plan was for us to take a train to Tientsin, then transfer everybody to a boat and sail to Hongkong. There we would all disperse and make our way to whatever country we were headed for. Easier said than done.

Eleven years after leaving Germany, I again found myself leaning out of a train window. This time I had to say good-bye to my parents who were still waiting for their visa for America. With the American consulate and most other foreign consulates by now closed in Shanghai, their future was very uncertain.

I had always enjoyed train travel, but there seemed to be so many tears and heartaches connected with it. Images of some other journeys flashed through my mind. Waving good-bye to cousins who fled Germany, leaving their parents behind never to see them again. Our trip to Czechoslovakia to visit my father's family, ending with everyone crying at the train station in Teschen when we left. Friends and relatives, whom we saw for the last time amidst the noise and smoke of the engines.

Being so young in those days I did not really understand the sadness and the tears, but now at age twenty, heavy with my unborn child, I knew, and now I cried for all the other times too.

32. MY GUARDIAN ANGELS

Fortunate to even find a seat I did not want to complain, but I felt tired and depressed. There was little room to stretch out on the hard bench. I could feel my legs gradually swelling up, as the overcrowded train sped through the Chinese countryside on the way to Tientsin. Shifting around uncomfortably in my seat, I paid little attention to the beautiful views unfolding beyond the window. Leafy green willow trees, their branches bending down into lakes and streams, farmers on their way home from the fields, children playing and waving at the train, all passed by as in a dream.

Already I missed my parents whose faces had faded away into the distance. My father unfailingly optimistic as always: "Keep smiling Illemaus, everything will work out for us all, believe me."

My mother trying to hold back her tears as she kissed me. When would I ever see them again? Why couldn't I be with them when I needed them so much? I felt very much alone, drifting along an unfamiliar path to an unknown future. Gloomily I wondered what life held in store for us.

Oleg in the meantime, was busily attending to our group's problems and trying to answer their questions. After he settled me in my seat, he checked on me from time to time to see if I needed anything. I managed to refrain from crying on his shoulder on those quick visits. Confused and frightened, some of the older people were already doing just that.

Our train was jammed with Chinese and foreign refugees. There were not enough seats for so many people, consequently quarrels started among the passengers and train conductors.

Loud complaints and arguments were directed at Oleg, the newly appointed group leader. He certainly had his hands full. No one paid any attention to me as I closed my eyes wearily.

"Come my dear, let us help you. Here, put your feet up on our laps, it will make you more comfortable." Soft voices came through to me.

Two nuns sitting opposite me smiled, as they lifted up my legs and massaged my feet. They got hot tea for me and rubbed my back. They were on their way back to their convent in Belgium, forced to leave behind the school and hospital they had built on foreign soil.

During our conversation, they told me about their childhood and the years spent working in the convent. With tears in their eyes, they shared their concern about the children they had left behind in the Chinese orphanage.

My husband and I had visited convent orphanages in Shanghai before we left. Famous for their knitted clothes and embroidery, we had bought some exquisite handmade outfits for our coming baby. All those were packed carefully in our suitcases, which were then thrown helter-skelter somewhere behind us into the baggage compartment of the train.

"You remind us of another woman long ago," they said gently. "She too had no place to lie down when her time came. She traveled many miles before she could rest and give birth to her child. It is a special privilege for us to be here now, to comfort you and help you on your journey."

I never forgot the two nuns. Almost like guardian angels, they appeared just when I needed them most. The little religious medal they gave me became part of my treasured possessions.

On arrival in Tientsin many hours later, we found ourselves assigned to a hotel called The Talati House. It was situated near the docks and was owned and operated by an Indian gentleman, his wife and numerous relatives. As a modest family type hotel, it was evident that they could not cope with repeated onslaughts of trainloads of refugees.

There was definitely not enough space for our group, so some of our people set up housekeeping in the lobbies and corridors. Other hotels in the area were equally jammed with people fleeing from China. We all just had to wait, until we could get passage on ships sailing to Hongkong, and try to make the best of it in the meantime.

Again out of the blue, a second band of good Samaritans in the shape of the Moalem family appeared. Sephardic Jews who had lived in Shanghai for years, they were also en route to Australia. Arriving a few days before us, they were waiting for a ship out of Tientsin. Oleg knew them well. He had grown up with Joe, Danny and Louise.

The entire family good-naturedly took me right under their wing. They found me forlornly sitting in the lobby, unable to get a room, my swollen, by now shoeless feet propped up on my luggage. I fought back tears of relief when they insisted that I sleep in one of their beds. Their sons and Oleg too, slept on the floor beside me. I was so thankful to stretch out and lie down in a real bed again, that I could not have cared less how many others were sleeping in the same room with me.

While Oleg was occupied the next few days arranging our group's passage out of Tientsin, I spent my time with the family. Mrs. Moalem made me take walks, talked to me, and fed me until I could not move. One of our favorite stops was a Russian bakery around the corner that sold the most fantastic pastries.

"Oh don't worry, it will all come off after you have the baby," my motherly friend insisted. I gave in quite easily, but of course I kept gaining even more weight. Even though I had several weeks to go, my rapidly increasing size suggested that a multiple birth might be imminent.

"I can't possibly get up there, why don't you go on the top and I'll go on the bottom. Just make sure you don't fall on me."

With definite misgivings, Oleg and I checked into our cabin on the *Heinrich Jenssen*, an old coastal steamer sailing out of Tientsin, bound for Hongkong. Six other people shared the cabin with us. Somehow we distributed our belongings on the floor or under the four sets of bunkbeds. It was a tight squeeze to get in and out of the cabin.

The nights were long and noisy with the accompaniment of loud snoring, grunting and coughing by our assorted cabin mates. Some of them talked in their sleep, others tossed and turned all night. Frequently there were some fierce arguments between one young couple that went on half the night, until the others yelled at them to stop.

Due to my advanced state of pregnancy, frequent trips to the bathroom were necessary. It always took me a while to awaken my sleeping husband in the top bunk, so he could accompany me to the bathroom located at the end of a long, dimly lit passageway.

Fortunately, as the weather was pleasantly warm, we spent most of the daylight hours outside on the deck. Sailing close to shore, we now had plenty of time to watch the beautiful Chinese country-side pass by, swathed in mist in the early mornings, only to emerge in startling beauty when the sun shone. Soft rolling green hills, valleys lush with trees and flowers, farmers working the land. It was a welcome sight for us as we sat on deck. Some of the young people passed the time singing songs, accompanied by others on guitars and harmonicas.

Sitting lazily in the warm sun, I began to feel some lifting of the tension and fatigue of the last few weeks. I tried to look at the future with a measure of optimism. This optimism, combined with a lack of squeamishness, was definitely needed in the dining room.

We got used to closely inspecting the food, which consisted mainly of fish. Hitting the bread against the table before we ate it, was always a good idea. An ant colony must have set up headquarters in the kitchen and they often appeared in our dinner. This encouraged me to rigorously cut down on my food intake. I was finally on a diet whether I liked it or not.

The *Heinrich Jenssen* steamed into Hongkong harbor about a week later. Passage for our continuing trip to Australia by sea, had been booked for us by the International Refugee Organization. We all got ready for the disembarkation maneuver. Our steamer dropped anchor in the middle of the harbor. It was necessary for us to climb down a swinging rope ladder along the side of the ship, to get into a ferry. Customs officials on the ferry were to check our papers one more time, before we would finally be escorted to our ship, anchored some distance away, and head for Australia.

"One step at a time, don't look down! Hold my hand, trust me, I won't let you fall." A reassuring voice kept repeating the words over and over. The rope ladder swayed under me as the waves washed up against the ship. My husband's arm was around me, a friendly passenger holding my hand, one step in front of us. Together, they maneuvered my descent off the *Heinrich Jenssen*. Quietly encouraging me, we all inched our way down slowly. The other passengers leaned over the rails, alternately shouting encouragement from above or holding their breaths to see if I would fall into the harbor. Heavy and clumsy, embarassed to be in such a conspicuous position, I was completely terrified. Quite unable to see my feet, let alone the steps in front of me, I was absolutely sure that I would come to a watery end.

Miraculously I made it down into the ferry. Unfortunately, at that point we found that more difficulties lay ahead. Not about to assume responsibility for a premature birth in transit, the Australian officials sent to process our transfer to their ship, took one look at me and absolutely refused permission for me to board.

Contact was hastily established with the I.R.O. and Lorenzo Lo in Shanghai, to come to the rescue. At the end of a long day, still not in possession of proper Hongkong landing papers, Oleg and I found ourselves ensconced as guests on a houseboat tied up at a pier in Hongkong harbor. That must have all come about due to the influence of Lorenzo Lo. We really were not sure, but I do know that we did not ask too many questions of the polite and helpful crew on the boat. We were more or less between the devil and the deep blue sea at that point. It became our home for the next few days, while efforts to get us on our way were made on our behalf, by the various authorities.

By chance, we were able to make contact with Sir Horace Kadoorie, my old time benefactor at the S.J.Y.A. school, when I first arrived in Shanghai. By 1950, he had already established his headquarters in Hongkong.

He invited Oleg and I to meet him at the Penninsula Hotel, sending a car to pick us up. While sipping English tea and eating dainty little sandwiches and petits fours in the elegant surroundings we suddenly found ourselves in, I tried to keep my shoes out of sight. My feet had become so swollen that I had cut the backs of my shoes off, so I could slip into them at least partially.

I told Sir Horace that I cheered the loudest, when he came on his bicycled inspection tours to our school. It made him laugh, and we all talked about old times.

Sympathetic to the predicament we found ourselves in, he used his considerable influence to help us. He not only sent me for a check-up to an obstetrician in Hongkong, who decided that it was quite possible that I could give birth early, with the way I was running about; but Sir Horace also arranged for airline tickets for us to fly to Sydney, via Singapore, within the week.

Leaving China behind us at last, we spent two days in Singapore at the Raffles Hotel for a much needed rest, before resuming our flight to Australia.

34. IT'S A GIRL

In spite of having lived for several years in Australia, Mrs. Sudakoff still spoke English with a heavy Russian accent. She had a habit of making lengthy speeches, liberally punctuated by heavy breathing. One of her favorite words was: *mhmm*, a melodic, humming sound appearing several times in every one of her sentences. Her present husband, Mr. Sudakoff, was a quiet little man, who succeeded three or four other spouses in his wife's matrimonial career. These two were our Australian sponsors.

Cajoled by my mother-in-law, Mrs. Sudakoff's longtime friend, they had agreed to sign all the necessary documents and had solemnly promised the Australian government to look out for us. Taking their duty very seriously, they ceremoniously came to meet us at the airport, when we arrived in Sydney, in May, 1950.

Poor, kind Mrs. Sudakoff. Attired in a flowery dress with matching hat, under which her round face covered with many layers of white face powder peered out, she was quite visibly upset when she saw me for the first time. Here I was, unmistakably pregnant, staggering off the ramp and coming at her like a ship in full sail. Not having any children of her own, she was quite taken aback by my abundant fertility.

Good-naturedly, they tried to make the best of things. This elderly couple slept on the kitchen floor of their tiny house in Lillyfield, New South Wales, and gave their only bedroom to us. As we soon found out, while we tried to sleep, the bedroom was shared not only by the two of us, but also by a contingent of Australian sandfleas, who fired off welcoming salvos throughout the night.

Shortly after our arrival, we found a room for rent with another Russian family. These people spoke nothing but Russian to each other. It effectively excluded me from any conversation in the house.

As we had very little money left, Oleg looked for odd jobs almost as soon as we arrived in Sydney. He also enrolled in Sydney Teachers College, to get his post-graduate teaching degree. Without this certification, he was not permitted to teach school in Australia.

Completely exhausted, he used to come home in the evening, first from his job as a ditch digger, then later as a welder of railway carriages in an iron foundry. Trying to keep his eyes open, he ate the dinner I had cooked for him.

This did not faze our ubiquitous landlady, who inundated him with a barrage of noisy conversation, the minute he sat down at the dining room table. I was allowed use of the kitchen, where I cooked under the landlady's critical eye and ongoing remarks in Russian to her husband, no doubt about my lack of skill. He had the sense to keep quiet, while attempting to disappear behind his newspaper.

On one memorable occasion we were almost thrown out of the house, when I went off to answer the telephone, leaving a tap flowing in the kitchen sink. The water overflowed onto the floor, into all the kitchen drawers, and on into the next room. That lady screamed at me in all the different languages she could think of.

I was very unhappy in those days, and in tears much of the time. I did not feel well at all and continued gaining more weight. When I went for a check-up to Crown Street Maternity Hospital, I was immediately admitted with toxemia. Put on medication and a diet, I lost five pounds. After a week I was discharged, went home and quickly gained the weight back again.

When I went into labor a few days later, Oleg was working on a construction job on a highway somewhere. I was unable to contact him. My landlady's son Nick, who spoke English and was the only one who was ever nice to me in that house, volunteered to drive me to the hospital.

For some time, I had been unable to wear my wedding ring because my fingers were swollen. This, together with the fact that the personable young man who carried my suitcase, identified himself as just a friend, when I registered at the hospital, raised some eyebrows among the very prim and proper Nursing Sisters who admitted me. This was, after all the year 1950, in what was still a rather old fashioned Australia.

Named after my two grandmothers, Jeanette and Rosa, beautiful blond, blue-eyed Jennifer Rose was finally born on June 23. Due to a long and difficult delivery, she was a forceps baby. It was three days before I actually got to see her.

I remember how upset and impatient I was, imagining all kinds of terrible things that could have happened to my baby. Then the Sister walked into the large room I shared with four or five other new mothers. From the several tightly wrapped little bundles she carried at the same time, I unerringly picked out the one that was mine. This was my baby and I knew exactly who she was.

35. NEW AUSTRALIANS

O n summer weekends, we always tried to get to the beach. Bondi Beach was a favorite of ours. It was at least an hour's travel time, so the trip usually turned into a complicated maneuver, involving much planning and packing.

It was quite out of the question for us to buy a car. We had a hard enough time making enough money just to cover our living expenses. As a matter of fact, neither of us even knew how to drive. This had never been a problem in Shanghai. There, for a small amount of money, we always had a rickshaw, pedicab or taxi easily available.

Now, living in one of the sprawling Sydney suburbs, things were a little different. Bags overflowing with towels, home-made baby-food, diapers, food and drink, collapsible strollers, first one and later two babies, were loaded onto buses, trams and trains for the long trek to one of the many beautiful sunny beaches around Sydney.

It was there, that we gathered with our old friends from Shanghai. While the men swam and played ball, the children played together in the sand by the water's edge, under our watchful eyes. The women sat and talked, there was always so much to discuss with each other. Often we wondered if we would ever have homes of our own.

Nearly everyone we knew, shared housekeeping with parents or in-laws. A financial necessity; but not always a blissful arrangement. It was those talks on the beach, or in each other's kitchens on wintery Sundays, over a shared lunch, when our friendships were cemented into solid relationships. It helped to put some of our common problems into the proper perspective.

Most of us went through the same difficult times, often living in multi-family homes with new babies, who sometimes turned night into day. We all had hard working husbands, who were well intentioned, but not always available when we needed them. Just knowing that we were all together, trying to get ahead and working toward the same goals, gave us a feeling of strength and confidence. As my father always used to say, there really was safety in numbers.

Some of our friends had fled to the Philippine Islands from Shanghai. From there, they accepted free passage and visaes to Australia, in exchange for work in the sugar cane fields for a specified period of time. On their long-awaited release, from what turned out to be an unexpectedly harsh existence, many of them settled down in Sydney, where they found jobs and started to raise their families.

All of us attempted to adjust to our new environment as quickly as we could. Australian customs and traditions were somewhat different from those we were used to. The locals liked to refer to us as *New Australians*. Although not actually unfriendly, they generally kept their distance for quite a long time, carefully retaining a kind of cautious reserve toward anyone different from themselves.

It took us a while to get accustomed to the Australian Sterling money system, the Australian-accented English heard in the streets, which caused some misunderstandings in the beginning, and to understand how the people lived. Their fascination with the local horse and dog races, warm beer drunk as quickly as possible before closing time at the local pub, and the intricacies of the national lottery system, eluded us totally.

On the other hand, it did not take us long to discover the fish and chips stores found on almost any corner. This was an Australian tradition, probably inherited from the English, or *Limeys*, as they were irreverently referred to. With a dash of vinegar added, fried fish and chips were wrapped steaming hot in newspaper, and usually eaten without benefit of silverware. Here was one local custom we happily adopted right away.

On weekends, when we did not go to the beach, we climbed on the top of the double decker buses with our children, and went sight-seeing in the suburbs around us. Sometimes we took the ferry that sailed around in Sydney Harbor, or spent the day with the children in Taronga Park Zoo. There were so many beautiful places to see, we tried to go to a different spot each time.

Oleg had a fairly easy time making friends with other students at the University. He had always felt at ease in a school atmosphere, and his outgoing personality soon won him new friends. I, on the other hand, depended heavily on my Shanghai girlfriends. Staying at home with the babies, did not give me many opportunities to make new friends or meet people, aside from a few neighboring mothers I saw in the park or at the Baby Well Clinic, where I took the children for their check-ups.

When Jennifer was just a few weeks old, we moved to a house on Gladstone Street, in Leichhardt, a suburb of Sydney. It was owned by Oleg's mother, who had arrived in Australia with his brother Igor shortly after we did.

On top of a hill, accessible by narrow stone steps, the house overlooked a valley. From our windows, we could see acres of red corrugated iron roofs, covering small family homes, that were surrounded by flowering gardens and tall waving palm trees. It was essentially a typical working class suburb. Each house, while not always having a number, usually boasted a name plate. A favorite name was *Emoh Ruo*. We finally figured out that it meant Our Home, spelled backwards.

I used to stand up there on the stone porch, usually with a baby sitting on my hip, and wave to Oleg, as he rode his bicycle up and down the hilly streets, on his way to the University.

Our little apartment consisted of two connecting rooms in the front of the house, with a tiny enclosed veranda that was covered by the ubiquitous corrugated red roof. The rain used to sound like beating drums on the roof. Sometimes it rained right into the room, when we had neglected to plug up the little holes above us. This porch became my kitchen, by virtue of the fact, that it had a gas ring and a small sink with cold running water. The sink had no outlet. Hidden behind my homemade curtain, the bucket placed underneath had to be carried out and emptied into the toilet. Sometimes on cold nights, I would cheat a little. Furtively, I tossed the water out into the front yard, hoping my in-laws would not look out the window.

Jennifer was a good and peaceful baby. She did not complain often, even in my inexperienced hands. She was sweet and affectionate but quite shy at the same time, not taking easily to strangers. But she always had a smile and a big welcome for her *Daya*, when he came home from work or school.

When she was twenty months old she was joined by a sister, whom we named Elizabeth Sandra. Eventually after some experimenting, she was henceforth called Sandy by the family.

She was quite the opposite of Jennifer who was fair skinned, had blue eyes and light blond hair. Here came Sandy with her dark curly hair, big brown eyes, a melting smile and something of a temperament when she did not get her own way.

I distinctly remember a feeling I had, right after she was born, in King George V Hospital in Sydney. After the nurse showed her to me, I was left alone. The lights were dimmed in the room. I felt enveloped in a cloud of euphoria such as I had rarely, if ever, known. It was very peaceful just lying there dreaming.

A while later, Oleg showed up with a bunch of flowers for me. In those days, husbands were not seen anywhere near the delivery room. This was woman's work, everyone agreed. Their mates waited around outside somewhere, until they were called in to congratulate themselves, and their wives, on this little miracle they had performed together.

It was a good thing I had had my one moment of euphoria. Once I got home there was little time to sit around day-dreaming. While Oleg was out working and studying all day and most evenings, I looked after the children, kept the rooms clean and did the washing, shopping and cooking.

"Where are my sunglasses? Do we have enough money for the fare? What happened to the baby's bonnet? We'll never get out of here at this rate."

While Jennifer helped collect our belongings, her little sister Sandy was just as busy unpacking everything again, the minute we finally had it stowed away.

Everywhere I went, I pushed the pram with the babies. Often the groceries were in it also. When we climbed up some of those steep hilly streets, Jennifer had to get out and walk, always holding on to the pram's side. From early childhood, our children were used to walking. A habit that stayed with them. As they got older, even a long hike never bothered them.

Once I had to visit the dentist to have a wisdom tooth extracted. Afterwards, I walked all the way home as usual, with the two children in the carriage. Fortunately, I arrived home about the same time that the anesthesia wore off.

There were two cribs in our bedroom now, jammed in beside our double bed and two dressers. Not much space to move about. I used to hang blankets over the side of the cribs, so the children could go to sleep quietly. This worked fairly well with Jennifer, who only peeked out from time to time to make sure we were still there. Sandy, however, refused to lie down, developing a habit of standing in her crib holding on to the bars. Not wanting to miss anything of interest, she would go to sleep standing up. I used to run and catch her, so she would not bang her head on the crib bars, when she finally fell down sound asleep.

In our living-dining room combination, we had a radio to which I always listened, while I was doing my housework. It sat on the mantle of the fake fireplace with the gas jets, which doubled as a heater and clothes drier, when it rained. I particularly liked an orchestral arrangement of *Wyoming*, which was often played. I knew Wyoming was somewhere in America. It might as well have been on the moon. That distant place held some kind of fascination for me. It always made me homesick somehow. Homesick for a place I had never seen. Many years later, thirty seven years to be exact, I found myself in Wyoming. But that's another story.

Behind the house there was a large garden, with fruit trees and flower beds. Lying in their prams, protected by the mosquito net that once was my wedding veil, our babies used

146

to go to sleep, looking up into glossy lemon leaves waving in the breeze.

When Oleg's mother had time off from her job in a cookie factory, she liked to work in the garden, tugging weeds and planting flowers, while Oleg mowed the grass. When Jennifer and Sandy got older they played in the garden, often chasing the resident chicken, whose infrequently laid eggs were always saved for them. I often think that was the place and the time, when Oleg first discovered his green thumb, his love for growing things. He certainly never had the opportunity to do any gardening in Shanghai, where he always lived in a single room, spending most of his spare time in the Y.M.C.A. pool and gymnasium.

All the way in the back of the garden there was a little hut containing the toilet, or W.C. (water closet) as it was called. On rainy nights we used a flashlight and umbrella on our trips to the outhouse. This arrangement was quite common in the area in those days.

On the side of the house, which she shared with Igor, my mother-in-law had her kitchen. She was the proud owner of a proper gas stove, complete with oven, in which I used to bake my cakes. There was also a large gas-heated kettle, called a copper, used to boil laundry. Next to that were deep wash basins, with old fashioned manual clothes wringers attached to them. After we did all our laundry by hand, including the babies' terrycloth diapers, everything was hung out on the line to dry in the sun.

In the corner of her kitchen, there was a bathtub, used by all of us. As far as our personal cleanliness was concerned, that would depend on how often, and how long, my in-laws were out of the house. Timing was of the essence, on the occasion of taking a bath. At least on my part. I was still dreaming of a little privacy somewhere in my life.

Once a week, we had dinner with Oleg's mother and his brother in their small dining area, off the kitchen. She always cooked a large leg of lamb, aware that we could not afford to buy it for ourselves. Often there were some homemade Russian specialties like *pelmeni, piroushkies* or a tasty *vinaigrette* along with it. It was from her, that I learned some of the old Russian recipes handed down in her family. Prominent among them were the *passkha* and *koolich* for Russian Easter. I still make them every year, according to the recipe copied from Alexandra Vassilievna in her Sydney kitchen.

36. ONCE MORE ON THE HIGH SEAS

While we were making a new life for ourselves *down under*, my parents embarked on a long round-about journey from Shanghai to America. The foreign embassies in China had closed by the year 1950, due to the Communist takeover; so my parents' only option as stateless persons, was to go back to Germany, where American authorities gradually processed their immigration documents.

My mother and father were not happy to find themselves living in a crowded refugee camp, sharing a room with another couple, waiting from day to day for a summons from the American Consulate. Worse than that, was the idea of being back in Germany, a place that held so many memories for them. Once it had meant security, a home and family, but by now all those ties were severed. Most of the family that stayed behind in 1939 had perished in the camps. There was nothing left to connect my parents with the life they had known years ago. They could not wait to leave it all behind them for the second time.

It took nearly a year for all the formalities to be concluded, while they lived in Foehrenwald Camp in the Black Forest. From far away Australia, I sent them food parcels and pictures of the grand-daughters they had never seen.

Eventually in 1951, my parents arrived in New York on an American troop-ship, and were happily reunited with Edith and Jim and their two young sons Steven and David. They moved in with Edith, who lived in Asbury Park, New Jersey, and helped her with the children. Jim was still in the army, serving in Korea. That left only me, half a world away, separated from all the others.

For years it had been my dream to go to America some day. It was always at the back of my mind. Life was not without hardship for us in Australia, and I suspected, that things would probably not be that much different in America, particularly in the beginning. But one thing I knew for certain, I did not want to live my life so far apart from my parents. I missed them too much.

With all the others now safely in America, we started working to make the dream a reality. Oleg was successful in obtaining a scholarship for graduate studies at Springfield College in Massachussetts, based on his years of Y.M.C.A. work in Shanghai. My parents found sponsors for us to enter the U.S.A. not as students but as immigrants, so that we could stay and eventually become citizens. They used all of their cash reserves to finance our trip. We certainly could not afford such an expense, we had a hard enough time just living from day to day.

I happily threw all my energy into the multitude of travel details, filling out endless documents, scheduling our medical check-ups, police clearances, packing our things, selling the furniture. A million details to take care of. While Oleg worked up to the last minute, I made the rounds every day, always with the children in tow. We spent hours at the shipping office, at the consulates, at the banks where my parents had transferred money. Tired and hungry, we returned home in the evenings, one step closer to departure.

"Wave to Granny. Here, you hold the streamers." Leaning over the rail, holding three year old Jennifer and seventeen months old Sandy, we waved and shouted good-byes. As the faces of Oleg's mother and brother, many of our old Shanghai friends, plus some new-found Australian friends, faded in the distance, the *Castel Verde* slowly moved out of Sydney harbor, trailing colored streamers and balloons.

The fact that the ship's name, translated into English was "Green Castle" sounded like a good omen to me. Green had always been my favorite color. *Sitmar* Shipping Company had arranged this special sailing to England as the ship's last voyage. Consequently the fares were lower than usual. We soon found out that the ship's hold was half empty. Therefore she tended to roll in the seas, often making Oleg and Jennifer seasick. Sandy and I on the other hand, blessed with stronger stomachs, never missed a meal. It was our first taste of Italian cuisine. We punctually showed up at mealtimes, quickly learning to sprinkle grated cheese on the simple and well cooked food.

Most of the passengers traveled in tourist class, as there were only a few private cabins on the ship. Men and women were housed in separate dormitories, below deck, with thirty or fourty double-decker berths in each. There were no cribs for the babies. I had to strap Sandy into her pram harness, attached around her waist and shoulders, and tie the straps onto the bed so she would not fall out while she slept. As I was afraid she would entangle herself if I left her alone, Jennifer and I went to bed at whatever time Sandy did.

We set up housekeeping, spreading ourselves out over two bottom bunks, quite cozily surrounded by our luggage, the children's dolls and teddy bears, our cans of dried milk and orange juice powder brought from Sydney, neatly in a row. There were also the wet diapers and clothes I had hand-washed, drying on the bedrails. It was so hot down there in the airless cabin, that the laundry usually dried overnight.

The three of us used to meet Oleg up on the deck and spend the days together. We walked the decks, played bingo or canasta, and cooled off in the little salt water swimming pool with the children. We always had our meals together, provided some of us were not seasick.

After a while, we added a little blond Dutch boy to our entourage. His mother was too seasick to take care of him, so we took him along with us to the upper decks. Jennifer spent much of her time watching out for him and Sandy. Then she would report to me what they were up to. She learned to take responsibility very early in her life.

The passengers' health became affected by the July heat, overcrowded cabins and less than perfect bathroom facilities. The ship's doctor was kept quite busy. There were many children on board. When one got sick with whatever was going around, they all caught it. We tried to keep our children close to us at all times and away from the others, but by the time we landed in Italy nearly four weeks later, Sandy had come down with a bad case of diarrhea. The medicine the doctor had given her worked so well, that she became constipated. She cried much of the time.

Our original travel plan was to sail to Europe, arriving in Italy in early August. We had tickets to go by train through France, across the English channel by ferry, on to London and then to Nottingham to visit my Uncle Ernest. From there we were to fly to New York, where my parents were to meet us.

It did not quite work out that way. Difficulties arose as soon as we stepped ashore in Genoa. We had an official travel document from the Australian authorities stating who we were and where we were going. But we were not Australian citizens, merely stateless refugees who had lived in

Sydney for three years. The Australian government would not back us if difficulties arose. We were strictly on our own.

The Italian Police refused to honor our travel documents containing our Italian transit visa. A nice young Italian policeman was assigned to watch over us, until we got on the train and left the country. Fortunately, he liked children, made friends with them right away, even teaching them some Italian words. He followed us around all day, making sure we would not stay in Italy illegally. We bid him farewell at Genoa's train station, much to the children's regret. They thought he had become a member of the family.

37. MY ACTING DEBUT

By late afternoon we finally settled ourselves in the train compartment. Jennifer carried her doll and Sandy clung to her teddy-bear, which like the rest of us, were beginning to show sings of wear and tear. The never ending can of Australian milkpowder, some fresh fruit and bread from the market in Genoa, were to keep us satisfied for a while.

There was an awful lot of confusion at the train station that day. Crowds of people were pushing and shouting, trying to get on the train all at once. It was only then we found out that a general strike had been declared in France. Our train would be unable to enter France. Instead it was re-routed to go through Switzerland, Germany and Holland.

This presented several immediate problems for us. We had no visa for travel through those countries, also we had only a small amount of cash with us for emergencies. But as we really had no alternative, we decided to just sit tight and hope for the best.

The train quickly became overcrowded. Every compartment was completely filled. People who could not find seats, were sitting on the floor in the passageway, adding to the confusion. The August heat affected everyone. Tempers were beginning to rise. It was not long before drinking water was in short supply. With so many people using the toilets at the end of each car, some of them overflowed, adding to the foul odors already present.

The dining car soon ran out of food and was disconnected from the rest of the train during the night. We were dependent of buying whatever food we could find at railway stations along the route. This being an unscheduled train, the stops were infrequent and of short duration. Afraid to leave the safety of the train, we just hung out the window, buying whatever was held up for sale by vendors running along the side of the slowly moving train.

We traveled through Switzerland during the night without incident. But it was too soon to congratulate ourselves. By the time we arrived at the Swiss-German border early the next morning, we watched German border police remove some of our fellow passengers who were unable to produce transit visas. Panic was just a step away. Knowing that we might be next, Oleg and I put our heads together to figure out what our options were.

During all this time, I was trying to comfort Sandy who was in considerable pain with her stomach problems. She had screamed loudly most of the night, no matter what I did I could not calm her. Oleg held Jennifer on his lap. She cried copiously in sympathy with her sister. Naturally this did not endear us to our fellow passengers. I am sure some of them were hoping that we would be removed from the train, and they could get some rest.

In the midst of all the confusion, I threw myself on the mercy of the police, when they informed us that we too would have to leave the train. I had no idea where we were or what would happen to us if we got off. I cried, I begged, I pleaded. In my hastily remembered German, I made a strong appeal to their sympathy to allow us to continue on and get Sandy to a hospital in England.

The strategy worked and we successfully repeated the same maneuver at the next border, this time with the Dutch police. I, who had wanted to be an actress when I was young, finally got my chance to put on a performance. Only this was no act, I was deadly serious.

As the train rolled into Holland I felt vastly relieved to leave Germany behind me. The sight of the German police on the train had brought back long forgotten feelings and memories of the time when we fled from Berlin. I was very uncomfortable just passing through Germany, and terrified of nearly being cast adrift there. Thinking of my parents, I could now understand how they must have felt on their return to Germany two years earlier.

By the time we made a bedraggled appearance at the Hook of Holland, the children were really exhausted. We were concerned for them both, particularly Sandy, who was nearing the end of her strength. The channel ferry was not scheduled to sail until the next morning. For a few anxious moments we thought we might have to sleep on the floor of a waterfront restaurant, where many other people from our train had bedded down. However, the friendly Dutch captain of the ferry anchored at the dock took pity on us, offering our family his own cabin to spend the night. He also ordered the ferry's pharmacist mate to give Sandy a sedative to calm her down.

Passing through Harwich customs on England's east coast the next afternoon, a sympathetic offical offered Sandy a glass of water. Stopping her crying just long enough to drink, she bit right through the thin glass. Fortunately she did not hurt herself, but she caused quite a commotion. The kindly official was obviously distressed.

After a three hour train ride through the English twilight, the first thing we did on arrival in London was to have Sandy admitted to St. Bartholomew's Hospital for Children. By that time the doctors and nurses there seemed like absolute angels to us. They were very kind and efficient. Sandy was suffering from intestinal problems and a severe case of exhaustion. Fortunately, the fact that we had very little money did not matter. Socialized medicine in England paid for everything, even for people like us who were just passing through.

Waiting for Sandy to recover, we stayed at a small boarding house on Oxford Street. We visited the hospital daily, and also did some sight-seeing in London with Jennifer. She was very concerned about her sister and kept asking for her. A week later we collected Sandy, a little paler and weaker but mercifully feeling much better.

We went on to Nottingham to visit my Uncle Ernst and Aunt Martel. It was my first reunion with them since 1938. They had one adopted child, Jeffrey, whom they adored. He played with Jennifer and Sandy in the garden of their house, while Oleg and I took advantage of some much needed rest. We caught up on old times with my uncle and aunt and were treated with love and kindness by them. After the long and difficult journey, it was very nice to just sit back and relax for a few days in Nottingham, before continuing on to New York.

W e had just arrived from London at New York's Idlewild airport. Many years later to be renamed John F. Kennedy Airport. It was Sunday, August 23, 1953. After passing through immigration and customs, I anxiously looked all around for my parents. Surely I did not forget what they looked like, since the last time I saw them in Shanghai three years ago. I was very close to tears. There was no sign of them.

Finally we contacted them by telephone. My mother's breathless voice came over the phone, my father in the background giving instructions: "Illemaus, you are finally here and we are not even there to meet you. We never got your telegram with the arrival date from England. Isn't this unbelievable! But don't worry, Pappi and I are leaving Newark right this minute to get you. Just wait right there, don't go anywhere."

I had to laugh in spite of everything. There was no place for us to go, even if we wanted to. After our phone call, we settled down to wait for their arrival. It was a typical New York summer day, hot and humid. Many of the airport stores were closed on Sunday. It did not make much difference to us. We had very little money left to buy anything. The children were tired after the long plane ride. Jennifer leaned against me on the bench, Sandy was half asleep in her stroller. Our frayed umbrella carried halfway around the world, finally stashed in a nearby trash can.

A man sitting opposite started a conversation with us. When he heard that it was our first day in America, he bought us each a *Coca Cola*. Ceremoniously making a toast welcoming us all to the United States, he wished us luck and prosperity. We were quite moved, but not too surprised. We had always heard that Americans were friendly and open-hearted to strangers. Here was the living proof.

After what seemed like hours, the long awaited reunion with my parents finally took place. The hugging and kissing, the tears of joy seemed to go on forever. Until that moment I don't think I was really aware of how much I had actually missed them.

It was the children's first meeting with their grandparents. They quickly learned to call them by the German names of Omi and Opa, the same way I did with my grandparents long ago. On the other hand, Oleg's mother in Sydney was always referred to as Granny by the children, in the Australian fashion.

We finally all disentangled ourselves and, as my parents did not own a car, piled into all modes of transportation in tandem with our children and belongings. Thus we proceeded to my parents' apartment on High Street in Newark, New Jersey. As we started to leave, our *Coca Cola* benefactor ran after us, waving our old discarded umbrella. In the confusion, he thought we had forgotten it. We must have looked like a regular safari, and a noisy one at that. None of us stopped talking all the way home.

My parents slept on the pull-out couch in the living room, giving Oleg and I their one bedroom, the children sleeping on cots in the same room. There was a large old-fashioned kitchen with a breakfast nook, two benches built into the wall with a table in-between. A hand embroidered tablecloth, a vase of flowers, my mother's well remembered touch. The children loved that spot, playing there for hours, coloring in their books, making cookies with my mother or playing games with my father. Out of the forgotten things of their childhood, this was one place they always fondly remembered later in life. All they had to do was walk into a diner somewhere, see the booths lined up, and the memories would return.

After our arrival, my parents took some time off from their jobs to help us get acclimated to our new surroundings. My father worked in an office as a bookkeeper, while my mother sold hats in a department store. Her customers were intrigued by what they thought was a French accent. She sold a lot of hats that way, never actually pointing out that her accent was really German.

My parents proudly initiated us into the American way of life. By the time we arrived they had overcome some of their newness in their adopted country. They had just begun to stop thinking of themselves as immigrants. As with most newcomers their understanding of American customs and expressions increased as time went on. For instance, the casual use of first names by people one hardly knew, was a little strange for all of us. We had been used to a more formal style of behavior, a more rigid set of rules.

Looking back, I think it must have taken me at least a year or more to feel comfortable with people, to fit into the fabric of American life as I saw it. I did not want to be different anymore, I just wanted to be like everybody else. This was the big melting pot I had heard so much about, and I was finally to become a part of it. Our transition was made easier by the fact that people in general were invariably friendly, always kind to the children and ready to help us in any way they could.

I was just so happy to finally be in the same place with my entire family that any problems that arose, financial or otherwise, were soon put in their proper perspective and therefore easier to overcome. As I often said to the children in later years: "We were never poor, we just did not have much money for a time, but we were always rich in spirit and family unity." And that was the big difference.

We marveled at our first supermarket shopping expedition. We window-shopped at the many wonderful stores. Walking for hours around town, there were so many things for us to look at. Television was a new and fascinating experience. Everything was fresh and new to us and we loved it. The children played to their heart's content in the park around the corner, happy just to run around after the long journey.

A bus ride to Asbury Park brought us to my sister Edith and her family. We had not seen each other for five years. What a reunion that was. Beside their two sons, she and Jim now also had a daughter, all of whom immediately jumped into the little backyard pool together with Jennifer and Sandy. The children had no trouble getting acquainted with each other, except that they all thought their new cousins talked funny. My girls had a slight Australian accent, while Steven, David and Janie's speech was definitely American.

39. SPRINGFIELD, MASSACHUSSETTS

Our first year in America was spent at Springfield College, where Oleg had his scholarship for post-graduate studies in Physical Education. It was the perfect place to become integrated into American life. There were not many foreign students at the college at that time. We were the first foreigners to move into the student trailer colony, along the banks of the Massassoit River. From the start we felt welcome and accepted by our neighbors. All of us were more or less in the same boat; raising young families, studying, working at whatever jobs we could find. It was reminiscent, to some extent, of the life we had left behind in Australia. We all had a lot in common with each other, consequently it was a close knit community where people watched out for one another.

With a few hundred dollars borrowed from our old Shanghai friend Moti Gidumal, we bought a used, rather worn out trailer, with an extra room built onto it. Even though it was a small place it was comfortable and sunny, with large windows facing the river and the woods beyond. I cooked our meals on a two burner gas ring in the tiny kitchen area. More memories of my kitchen in Sydney.

Next to our fold down couch in the living room, stood a potbelly kerosene stove. One night when it refused to work in sub-zero temperature, the young student elected as Mayor by the trailer residents, came to our aid with a few volunteers. They worked for hours in the cold to repair the stove. In the meantime, Jennifer and Sandy slept soundly together on the army cot they shared, one at each end, warmly covered by all our blankets and coats.

We were busy all the time. Oleg attended classes and also worked, cleaning houses for a dollar an hour, lunch was included if he was lucky. I bought an old manual typewriter, set it up on a folding table in the trailer and took in typing from college students. I got paid by the page, frequently I also corrected their spelling free of charge.

Once, my Aunt Liccie and Uncle Erwin visited us from Boston. My aunt had learned to drive by that time. She was always liberally assisted with constant advice and instructions by her husband, who sat with maps in hand, in the passenger seat of their beloved car. Minutes before they arrived, the floor in the trailer kitchen gave way. Hastily erected wooden boards covered by an old rug, saved the lunch party I had prepared for them.

Day or night in all kinds of weather, often wearing our bathrobes, we got used to walking down the road leading to the Community Building, to use the bathrooms, take showers and do our laundry. On Sundays everyone gathered at covered dish suppers in the recreation room. The children had a wonderful time, there was always someone to play with.

We were invited to our first Thanksgiving dinner by a Russian born professor at the college, Dr. Peter Karpovich. For the first time we tasted turkey, cranberry sauce and all the traditional dishes prepared by the lady of the house. It was a very gracious introduction to a truly American holiday.

The professor had taken a liking to my husband. He used to interrupt his lectures to speak Russian with Oleg, usually jokes at which they both laughed uproariously. In the meantime, the class just had to wait for him to get back to the subject at hand.

Dr. Karpovich also came to the rescue, one rainy night, to drive Sandy to the hospital. Every time we asked her where her pennies were, she would point to her mouth and cough. As she was usually full of mischief, we just knew that she must have stored them in her mouth and swallowed them. Hours later, after we all came home again from the Emergency Room, she crawled under the bed and brought out the missing coins. She must have wondered what all the fuss was about.

I bought a rocking horse at a second-hand store in Springfield. It was to be a joint Chanukah-Christmas present for the children, after I cleaned and painted it. Unfortunately the only place where I could think to hide it, was on the flat roof of our trailer. When the time came to give it to the children, I knocked myself out and loosened some of my teeth, when I overbalanced and fell from the roof, while lifting it down by myself.

We have some happy memories of our first holiday season there, even though my face was still a little black and blue. The children were thrilled anyway; they received more toys from our neighbors in the trailer colony than they had ever seen before in their lives.

Things did not go smoothly all the time though. That winter we noticed that our Jennifer was pale and listless, showing little evidence of her usual sunny disposition. Obviously something was wrong. She was to spend several weeks in Springfield Hospital with a kidney infection. I don't think we realized at the time how seriously ill she actually was.

Sandy and I got on the bus and visited her every day. While Sandy became the darling of the waiting room staff charming everyone with her smile, I would go upstairs and sit with Jennifer. Whenever Oleg could get away he would come also. He always succeeded in making Jennifer laugh. When we left she always cried, and I did too. After she came home again she had to stay off her feet for a month, not an easy task for a three and a half year old. I just wrapped her up in blankets and tucked her into Sandy's wicker stroller, bought at the Springfield Salvation Army store. Now it became Sandy's turn to walk, holding on to the stroller whenever we went out.

In spring, Oleg also became a patient at Springfield Hospital, suffering from a skin infection on his hands. After studying and working very hard, combined with worries about money and our future, he had become run-down and tired. Now, with his hands bandaged, he was becoming quite impatient as well.

Again, the children and I took the bus every day, all of us carrying a home cooked treat and fresh clothes for him. I lined the girls up on the street outside, so he could wave to them from his window.

While he was recuperating, a call came from the Atlantic City Y.M.C.A. with a job opening for Oleg. They offered him Four thousand dollars yearly, to be their Physical Education Director. Four thousand dollars! We could not believe it. That was more money than we had ever seen. It made him feel better very quickly. He accepted immediately. At the end of the spring semester we sold the trailer, said good-bye to all our friends and off we went to Atlantic City.

40. ON THE JERSEY SHORE

New Jersey became our home. Looking back now it seems that the years passed quickly. Maybe too quickly. Five years after our arrival in America, we became United States citizens at a ceremony in Mays Landing, New Jersey. Rose Arnold and Billy Austin, two good friends from the Atlantic City Y.M.C.A. stood up with us, proudly acting as our sponsors.

Oleg worked at the Y.M.C.A. for four years and then went into the Public Schools of Absecon, New Jersey. There he remained busy and content, teaching Physical Education for the next twenty-five years.

In the meantime our family was growing fast. Shortly after our arrival in New Jersey in 1954, we had a third child, Nina Sharon. She was followed by our fourth daughter, called Irene Ann, in 1957. Our son, Peter Oleg, arrived a year later.

I had always promised myself that if I ever had a son, he would be named after my cousin Peter, whom I met just once when I visited Czechoslovakia as a child. I found out many years later that my cousin Peter, and also my cousin Herbert, both died at age fourteen in a concentration camp, in the final weeks of World War II.

Whenever the whole family went out anywhere, we always used a buddy system so we would not lose any of them. Jennifer always held Nina's hand, Sandy was in charge of Irene, while Oleg or I tried to keep up with Peter. We liked to call ourselves *The Original Seven*.

It was when Peter was just a baby, that we bought our first house in Brigantine, New Jersey. At last we left behind us a series of small rented apartments. Now there was enough room for all of us. The two older girls and the two younger girls each shared a bedroom on the second floor of the Cape Cod style house, Peter's room was downstairs next to ours. Into a corner of the big backyard, we put a sandbox and a swing set donated by friends of ours. One of the smaller attic spaces was fixed up as a private retreat for Nina and her dolls, when she wanted to get away from all the noise in the house. Living next to the beach, we spent many happy hours with the children there. On a summers night we could hear the roar of the surf through the open windows.

I used to walk around the house at night and check on all my children sleeping in their beds. It always gave me a good peaceful feeling, and I would climb into my bed contented with life.

With five children to support on a teacher's salary, we lived very simply, doing without luxuries. In the living room we had an ancient radio my parents had given us and an equally outdated television set. We used to bang on it when the picture faded out. I sewed a lot of the children's clothes, and did all the cooking and baking at home. We rarely ever went to a restaurant or to a movie, except to drive-in movies, with all the children giggling in the backseat. Family parties were in the form of picnics or backyard barbecues, with homemade entertainment put on by the children. We always watched out for sales, and were not too proud to accept gifts of outgrown clothing from friends.

When we bought our first car, a second-hand Buick, the children were so excited they ran up and down the street to tell their friends about it. They, in turn, could not imagine what all the noise was about. Most of them already had two cars in the garage.

Oleg did part-time coaching beside his regular teaching job. He became quite well known in sports circles around South Jersey. During the summers, I worked as a waitress in Atlantic City boardwalk restaurants to make some extra money. Often Oleg and I would meet coming or going to work. We tried to work out our schedules so that one of us was always at home with the children. Sometimes when that was not possible, Jennifer was put in charge of the younger children. They all learned to pitch in when necessary, to help around the house, not to fight with each other excessively - at least not within my hearing - and do their chores without too many complaints.

Many weekends and on holidays we exchanged visits with my sister and her family, which now included four children. The youngest one, Holly, was born a week ahead of Peter. Our old friends Moti and Eve Gidumal with their three children were also frequently in our house, or we in theirs.

I had also become fast friends with Barbara Moskowitz, my neighbor in an apartment complex in Margate, where we all lived for a while when the children were small. She and I spent countless hours on the telephone late at night, when all was quiet in the house. It became a nurturing, supportive source of strength for both of us, an important part of our lives, which has lasted over the years.

In those days my parents visited us quite often, as did my aunt and uncle from Boston. Once in a while, as a special treat, I got on the bus and went to New York all by myself, armed with a complimentary bus ticket from my parents.

They used to meet me at the Port Authority, and take me to lunch at a *Horn & Hardart Automat*. What fun we had putting the coins in and pulling out some unusual dish we never made at home, like clam chowder or pecan pie. Sometimes they would take me to see the show at Radio City Hall. Then we would take a bus to Leonia, where my parents lived then. Later on after both retired, they moved to Ventnor to be near us.

After two days of letting them totally spoil me, I climbed back on the bus with my mother's little package of sandwiches and fruit, not to mention a generous piece of marzipan, so I should not starve on the way home. I usually gained a few pounds on those visits.

Oddly enough, I often got headaches during the weekends with my parents. Maybe I tried too hard to relax and enjoy myself. I just was not used to all this attention anymore. I had become the one to always look out for others, not the other way around. Usually I worried how the family survived without me at home.

They, in the meantime, managed quite well of course. Generally eating all the food I had prepared ahead for them in one day, then existing on oatmeal, applesauce, bread and butter the rest of the weekend. They were aided and abetted by their father, who, taking advantage of my absence, would with his usual enthusiasm pull a mattress onto the living room floor, so they could do tumbling and gymnastics to their heart's content.

41. FAMILY TALES

I am in the kitchen, preparing dinner for just the two of us. The children are all grown now and have gone their different ways. I gave up my part time job as medical secretary, about the same time Oleg retired from teaching in 1984. Since then we have done some traveling, visiting friends and relatives all over the world, attending reunions of the old Shanghai crowd.

Oleg and I had a memorable visit in Russia with my husband's aunt Vera Vassilievna, the year before she died. We were joined there by my brother-in-law Igor and his wife Diana, who flew in from Australia. Aunt Vera lived out her life peacefully in the mountains of Kazakhstan, after spending sixteen years in a Soviet prison camp in Karanganda, during Stalin's time. I taped the stories she delivered in her high-pitched Russian speech. She was nearing ninety, but one could still sense the spirit and determination that had kept her alive against all odds.

There is enough time now for hobbies and doing things, together and separately, things we have always wanted to do. Oleg plays tennis and has learned to ski. I write, enjoy my yoga and take daily walks on the Ventnor boardwalk. Both of us work at our computer. We take courses at local colleges in subjects that interest us, we work around the garden and the house.

The realization that the hard days are finally over has opened up new possibilities. Now we are looking at what is known euphemystically as the golden years. We are going to find out if that is what they really are.

We have lived in Ventnor for 27 years now. Two people

rambling around in a three story house. Of course there is green-eyed Jade, a worthy successor to Clyde, who went to cat heaven after keeping us company for sixteen years.

Originally there were six bedrooms here in this big old house near the beach and boardwalk. An extra two bedroom apartment in the basement, was used as a summer rental for many years.

The house was always full. Every bed was taken, especially in the summers, when relatives and friends came to visit. There was always a lot of noise and laughter, and of course the usual arguing about who did what to whom and why. And always a lot of cooking and cleaning, plus tons of laundry. Sometimes it seemed as if we were running a rooming house, with the fresh sheets barely on the beds, before the next contingent of summer visitors rang the doorbell. The sand trekked in from the beach always underfoot, towels and beach chairs scattered all over the back yard. The ping-pong table was constantly in use, as was the dining room table on which a jigsaw puzzle was always spread out. In the summers we always had our meals either on the large front porch on the long banquet table, or out on the back patio off the kitchen, depending on how many people were here at the time.

Nowadays our life is a little simpler and quieter, and in the winters at least, not as hectic as it used to be. We enjoy the peace and calm. Most of the time. We are just a short walk from the ocean. Every day just like in the old days, we go down to the beach just to see if the ocean is still there. It is. It will be.

I have come a long way from 5l Chusan Road, where our family of four lived in one room when I was a girl. I have come a long way since then and sometimes I think I learned a lot along the journey and sometimes I think quite the opposite.

As time goes on, I find myself remembering the old days more often, realizing again and again how fortunate we are to have come this far, how blessed my children are to have grown up the way they did in this country.

We are grandparents now. Our oldest daughter Jennifer and her wonderful husband David have two sons, Alexander and Lucas. They used to come with the boys every year to spend part of the summer with us at the seashore. Now that Jennifer and David are busy with their careers and the boys are older, they fly here by themselves from Florida to spend a few weeks of their summer vacation with us.

The first thing they usually do is to check out the house and hope we did not make too many changes. They like things here to be exactly the way they remember them from the year before. Late at night before he goes to sleep, Alexander pours over our old family photo albums. Lucas once told me he likes it here because it is so old fashioned. Maybe they will remember that feeling when they get to be my age, the same way I remember my grandmother's potato soup. They are both handsome all-American boys and we are so proud of them.

Then there is our Sandy with her sparkling brown eyes, all grown-up now, who has done so well for herself in everything she undertakes. She is a poised, articulate and highly intelligent young woman with a terrific sense of fun and adventure. Always ready to plan and carry out a family celebration, she has been the spark of many a memorable feast, when all of us would gather together here at the house on Surrey Avenue.

Next in line came Nina, our middle child, and the first one to be born in the United States. A beautiful person both in mind and body, full of love and generosity for her family and

172

the whole world. As she grew older, she let her inner sense of peace and tranquillity become more dominant. One could feel a quiet strength and determination in her. Slim and graceful, with long shiny brown hair, she became known as Dona Nina while she lived on a ranch in Palenque. Nina had moved to Mexico with her daughter Natasha after her marriage to Nathan ended. A new life now opened up for her, together with Manuel as her loving companion. As a team they worked the land and lived off the harvest of the ranch. They were able to attain the simple meditative lifestyle they both favored. Natasha blossomed in that environment. In December 1983, Nina gave birth a beautiful brown-eyed son named Votan.

The fourth of our daughters, Irene, lives in Washington State with her husband Stephan. Irene is a sensitive, warm and caring person and was lucky enough to find a husband who shares those qualities. As the youngest of four girls, Irene seemed to be in a more comfortable position than some of the others. Not being the oldest or the youngest child for very long, she just fit right into her special niche in the family. With her bright smile and quiet temperament, she was rarely the instigator of any sibling upheavals. At least that was my impression, but I could be wrong. In later years the kids sometimes told me stories of their exploits at home. Much of what I heard was completely new to me. It always made us laugh how we all remembered things differently. Now that Sandy has also moved out to Seattle, she and Irene are not only sisters, but also best friends.

Shortly before this book went to press, Irene and Stephan became the proud parents of a beautiful baby boy. They named him Max.

And finally there is Peter, our only son. He looks very

much like his father, except that he is even taller and broader, but every bit as handsome. Peter was a star of the crew team at Atlantic City High School, became a lifeguard on the Ventnor beaches and is also an avid surfer. He is the only one of our children still living in Ventnor. He joined the Navy for three years and is now an Air Traffic Controller for the F.A.A. His wife, the beautiful Susanna, whose Italian heritage is being passed on to their daughter Celina, is a welcome addition to our multi-national family. Celina is our only grand-child who lives nearby, and we are happy to say she frequently comes roaring full speed to our house, to visit Pop and Grandmom. She spends hours playing with Pop, who has just as much patience with her as he had with his own children.

The last time our whole family was reunited, was in the summer of 1984, at Oleg's retirement celebration from the Absecon School system. A short time later Nina died in an automobile accident, together with Votan. She was only twenty-nine years old. It is the one thing in my life that I still have difficulty coming to terms with. She is never out of my thoughts. In my heart I will always miss her and her sweet baby. It is a sorrow that knows no end.

Since that time our grand-daughter Natasha has lived with her father in upstate New York. We are fortunate to have a close relationship with her and Nathan, with many visits to each other's homes. We are closely involved in Natasha's life and it is a source of joy and satisfaction for us. She shows every sign of becoming as beautiful and warm a human being as her mother was.

MEDITATIONS

Five cats sit on the window ledge
they do not speak,
but wait in silence,
green eyes staring
in the dusk of another day.

Where are you? The dreams
that went astray,
what happened to the time
there was to spare
and the songs we never sang?

Four cats sit on the window ledge
alone, not touching,
wrapped up in themselves.
One lies beneath the frozen ground
in the garden by the tree.
Eternal sleep, it's called
or some such fantasy.

No matter now, in spring
sunflowers and daisies
and maybe even butterflies.
The time is past for wishful thinking
of things that cannot be.
The cats sit on the window ledge,
to be joined one day by me.

More than fifty years ago, Edith and I had hoped to go to Israel to live on a kibbutz. We had fond visions of living on the land, planting and hoeing, wearing little sunhats to guard us from the hot sun. That was long before it became the State of Israel. We were going to join the *Aliyah* of children being sent out from Germany, sent out to safety when all other avenues of escape were closing. We did not go to Israel then. Instead we went to China together with our parents. It became a vague dream I never quite forgot.

We made that dream come true in 1992. It had always been my father's hope that one day he also would visit Israel. That wish never became a reality. By the time he had the means to travel, his health was was beginning to fail. My mother was not a good traveler; she did not like to go too far away from home when she became older. My father of course would not leave her, even when he was still physically able. He would never think of going anywhere without her, so the result was that they both stayed at home. He often told us that some day we should go to Israel for him.

My father died in 1974. A few months before his death, he started to write a diary recalling his youth in Czechoslovakia. Some years later, I deciphered his shaky handwriting, and translated his recollections from German into English. He died as he had lived, everything neat and tidy, leaving his stamp collection in perfect order, and all his papers and documents filed away alphabetically. He and my mother had bought a little house and retired near us in Ventnor. His last years were peaceful and happy.

My mother lived another thirteen years by herself in the same house. Until she became ill she carried on her usual life style. Always carefully dressed and wearing her sensible walking shoes, she got her exercise by walking all over town. She marched for miles on the Ventnor boardwalk, usually stopping at my house for a cup of coffee and a short visit before returning home. Pulling her little shopping cart behind her, she became a familiar sight at the local stores and the public library. She liked to do her own gardening and insisted on mowing the lawn herself. I used to watch her, standing out in the yard, feeding the birds until they got big and fat. She enjoyed her grandchildren and continued cooking her healthy german-style meals. As far as I am concerned, no one has ever been able to duplicate her *wiener schnitzel*. When she finally succumbed to the effects of senile dementia, it was a dreadful tragedy to see how she gradually slipped away from reality, slipped away from us and from herself.

My Aunt Liccie and Uncle Erwin had passed away some years ago, but after my mother died I realized that suddenly I had become the older generation. I began to feel that I wanted my life to have had some meaning. My childhood was not uneventful, to say the least, and I wanted to share my story with my children and my grandchildren. I wanted them to know where they came from, who we were and who our people were. Perhaps that was the time when I started to think about writing this book.

All those little stories my father used to tell us, went way back into old family histories. I am sorry now that I did not ask more questions of my parents, and get more details about the family and the old days. But when you are young and busy raising your own family, you just go one step at a time dealing with life on a daily basis. Such discussions do not often get the time and attention they deserve.

Now it is too late and I cannot ask my parents any longer. Even when they were alive, there were some things that were never discussed in the family. Maybe they were too painful and brought back too many sad memories for them. I can hear my father saying: "Don't worry your head about things you cannot change, let it rest." Yet I know he did not let it rest, and being his daughter I apparently did not either.

That is why this trip to Israel turned out to be more than we bargained for. Our group consisted of Edith, her son Steven, her daughter Holly and myself. Of course we saw all the sights from Tel Aviv to Jerusalem, Yad Vashem, the other museums and the beaches. We went to Massada, to the Dead Sea, to Lake Kinnereth and the Galilee. We talked with the people and saw how they lived. We felt at home. But one of the highlights of the whole thing was the reunion with our cousins.

There was my cousin Otto Borger and his wife Yehudith, both of whom I had met just twice over the last fifty years. Here was a man who somehow had survived ten concentration camps during the war, who came out with absolutely nothing left. A man who had picked himself up and made a whole new life in Israel. He is my father's sister, Hermine's son, the only one of his family to have survived the Holocaust. We spent a lot of time talking about the family. His sister Lydia whom we had played with in Teschen years ago, as well as our other cousins, all gone. Our grandparents Adolf and Rosalie Kohn and most of their children and grandchildren had disappeared in the camps, never to return.

So here we all sat in Otto and Yehudith's Netanya home,

being wined and dined, and I see a blue crystal wine glass on the shelf. Just one glass. It is the same type of long-stemmed glass that we had on our dining room buffet in Berlin. He explains that it belonged to our grandparents, who gave it to a neighbor for safekeeping, just before they were taken away to a ghetto in Wadowice, Poland. After the war, when Otto went back to Teschen to visit what was left of his old home, the blue crystal glass was returned to him.

Not far from Haifa, in Kiryath Bialik, my cousin Heinz-Seew Kohn lives with his wife Deborah. We both look a little different from the time I sat in his house with my grandmother, eating marzipan cakes at his Bar-Mitzvah celebration. We catch up on old family history. I am recording everything on my little tape recorder. We are talking in English and in German, with asides in Hebrew from Heinz to Deborah, who is busy bringing out more coffee and cake for us. It is now his first language but they talk too fast, and I with my schoolgirl Hebrew, cannot follow.

We wonder whether my grandparents Philip and Jeanette Mueller and Heinz's parents ever saw each other again, after they were all sent to Theresienstadt. We will never know. Heinz like many thousands of others like him, is still searching for his parents and his sister, even though he knows he will never find them again.

I left Israel with a feeling of having in some way tied up loose ends. Seeing a Kohn family likeness in Otto's face, noticing a hint of a smile on Heinz that reminds me a little of my grandfather Philip, some of their gestures and faintly European style conversation brings me right back to my childhood. I feel I am still a little girl, sitting at the table in my grandparents' house, listening to my uncles and aunts all laughing and talking at the same time. The candles lit and the wine poured, chicken soup served after the blessings were said at Passover, Rosch Hashanah or some family celebration. That's what I remember.

I suppose, in the end, that is what families are all about. Whether they all live together in the same country, or are scattered all over the world, like ours. We are all linked by the common thread of nurturing the body with the food we love to make each other eat, but more importantly than that, we are linked together, one generation after another, by our thoughts, by our memories and by an ever continuing love.

My parent's wedding, Berlin, 1926.

My sister and I, in garden of Siegmundshof 13, Berlin, 1938. pg. 30

My father's Fremdenpass, (stateless I.D.) pg. 34

My mother's Fremdenpass, (stateless I.D.) pg. 34

My father's parents with my parents and two uncles. Czechoslovakia 1927. pg.16

My father's medals from World War I. pg. 34

My paternal grandparents, Adolf and Rosalie Kohn. Czechoslovakia

My maternal grandparents, Philip and Jeanette Mueller. Germany

Genehmigung vom Innen-Ministerium vom _____ 19___ No.___

Kehlt noch!

PHs. VAN OMMEREN (BERLIN) G. M. B. H.   No.: 1113

GENERALAGENTUR DER
N. Y. K.-LINIE
(NIPPON YUSEN KAISYA)
TEL.: 12 22 73

BERLIN NW 7, den *17. Febr.* 1939
UNTER DEN LINDEN 24
(HAUS DER SCHWEIZ)

PASSAGE-AUFTRAG von: _____

für Herrn / Frau	Max **KOHN**	Fam.-Stand: *verh.* Beruf: *Kaufmann* Alter:	21.2.93 — 45
	Olga **KOHN** *Berlin N.W.87*		27.3.04 — 35
	Edith **KOHN**		8.5.23
	Ilse **KOHN** *Sigmundshof 13* Tel.: 52 1584		29.12.29

Adresse am Reiseziel: *Shanghai*

Reisepaß No. *3/35* ausgestellt am *11.7.35* in *Berlin* Art: _____
K/2/24
K 436/38 *16.1.34 Berlin*
Visum No. *K 437/38* ausgestellt am *20.2.39* in *Berlin* Art: _____

Per Dampfer / MS	Linie:
am:	
ab:	
nach:	
Klasse: Deck:	
Kabine: Bett: Preis:	
Zuschlag:	
anschließend Eisenbahnfahrt	
von: nach:	
zahlbar in $ Preis:	
und N. Y. K.-Linie:	
M. S.: *Kashima* Maru 70 Dampfer: Reise No.:	
am: *11.5.39* ab: *Neapel*	
nach: *Shanghai*	
Klasse: I Deck:	
Kabine: 23, 24 Bett: alle Preis:	
Zuschlag:	
Steuer (U.S.A.) Bordgeld *25.2. RM 200*	
Anzahlung am:	
Gezahlt $ _____ am:	
Bleibt zu zahlen:	

PASSAGE-ABRECHNUNG					
$	abz. %	= $	Kurs	Reichsmark	
			19		
3 Passagen					
	79.—				
	79.—				
	79.—				
$ 237.—		= RM		2844.—	
		= RM			

Besondere Wünsche:

NIPPON YUSEN KAISYA BERLIN AGENCY
PHS. VAN OMMEREN (BERLIN) G.M.B.H.
BERLIN NW 7, UNTER DEN LINDEN 24
TELEPHONE: A 2 FLORA 2273
Unterschrift

Richtigkeit der Fahrscheine vorbehalten.

**Speditions-Auskünfte
und -Aufträge hier.**

Lufthansa-Flugscheine hier erhältlich.

Invoice from N.Y.K. Line for journey on Kashima Maru to Shanghai, 1939. pg. 37

Our family on Kashima Maru, en route to Shanghai. 1939

Children's tea party on Kashima Maru. Edith and I are on top left side. 1939

In the garden, 69 Macgregor Road, Shanghai, 1941.
Left to right: Aunt Liccie, Uncle Erwin, Edith, my mother, my father, and I.

Our family in our room in the ghetto, 51 Chusan Road, Shanghai, 1944. pg.74

My mother, my sister and I ready for our walk. Shanghai 1944. - pg. 91

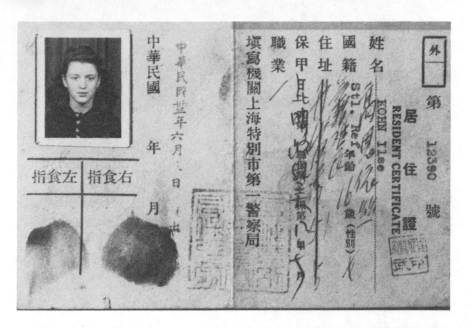

My Resident Certificate issued by Japanese, with yellow stripe on top right. pg.71

Garden Bridge, Broadway Mansion in background. Shanghai. pg.53

Betty walking on Nanking Road, past soldier on bicycle, and traffic cop. 1948

The Race Course, with Y.M.C.A. and Park Hotel in background, Shanghai. pg.52

Our wedding day, November 20, 1948. Shanghai.

Myself at age nineteen. Shanghai.

My children and I on New Jersey beach in winter, 1962.
Left to right: Peter, Betty, Nina, Irene. Jennifer and Sandy stand against fence.

My children and I in our garden, Brigantine, N.J. 1960.
Left to right, front row: Irene, Peter, Betty, Nina. Back row: Jennifer and Sandy

"The Original Seven" at Irene's wedding, New Jersey, 1980.
Left to right: Peter, Sandy, Jennifer, Irene, Nina, Betty, Oleg.